MW00781234

FROM *Wags* TO RICHES

FROM *Wags* TO RICHES

KIM KAPES

LIFESUCCESS PUBLISHING, LLC
8900 E. Pinnacle Peak Road, Suite D240
Scottsdale, AZ 85255

Telephone: 800.473.7134
Fax: 480.661.1014
E-mail: admin@lifesuccesspublishing.com

978-1-59930-128-0 (hardcover)
978-1-59930-239-3 (softcover)
978-1-59930-236-2 (ebook)

Cover :   LifeSuccess Publishing
Layout: Lloyd Arbour & LifeSuccess Publishing

COMPANIES, ORGANIZATIONS, INSTITUTIONS, AND INDUSTRY
PUBLICATIONS: Quantity discounts are available on bulk purchases of
this book for reselling, educational purposes, subscription incentives, gifts,
sponsorship, or fundraising. Special books or book excerpts can also be created
to fit specific needs, such as private labeling with your logo on the cover and a
message from a VIP printed inside. For more information, please contact our
Special Sales Department at LifeSuccess Publishing.

Cover Photo and Author Page Photo Credits:
Julie Fletcher, Orlando, Florida
JFletcher@orlandosentinel.com

Author Head Shots Credit:
Judy Tracy, Orlando, Florida
www.judywatsontracy.com

Printed in Canada

DEDICATION

A very special thanks to my family for their support and belief in me and all my endeavors.

To Ellen for all you have given, for your belief and strength.

To Sherri for the belief in the project and support all along the way.

I would like to thank all the great people at LifeSuccess Publishing who worked so hard to help me bring this book from concept to print.

A great big thank you to Quinci and Tony, Jimmy, Cassondra, Jennifer, and especially Erline for helping me and the animals at "In Harmony with Nature."

A special note to Carolyn, my friend, you are always in my thoughts.

To Jan and Glenn and the Dog Listeners around the world for your most special support and belief in me.

To all my friends who shared their stories.

Of course, thanks to my Navarre and all my "kids" that I love so much for helping to teach and guide me, and for their boundless lessons and patience.

JUST A DOG

(Excerpts taken from Richard A. Biby of Broken Arrow, Oklahoma)

"From time to time, people tell me, lighten up, it's just a dog or that's a lot of money for just a dog." They don't understand the distance traveled, the time spent, or the costs involved for just a dog. Some of my proudest moments have come about with just a dog. Many hours have passed and my only company was just a dog, but I did not once feel slighted…

If you too, think it's just a dog, then you will probably understand phrases like just a friend, just a sunrise, or just a promise. Just a dog brings into my life the very essence of friendship, trust, and pure unbridled joy…

I hope that someday they can understand that it's not just a dog, but the very thing that gives me humanity and keeps me from being just a man. So the next time you hear the phrase "Just a dog", smile because you know they just don't understand.

This book will show you that there truly is much more to our canine companions than being *"just a dog."*

Table of Contents

PREFACE

My life is far from normal. My family would be the first to agree with me. I do not follow the crowd and have always looked at things differently. I love my life and would not change one thing. I would like to share a bit of my life with you in the following pages to help you on your journey. I have a strong connection with the following quote, and I would like to share it with you:

"Be daring, be different, be impractical, be anything that will assert integrity of purpose and imaginative vision against the play-it-safers, the creatures of the commonplace, the slaves of the ordinary."

– Cecil Beaton

One of those differences in me has been with animals. I have always loved animals and felt a special connection with them. When I was a child, my family would visit zoos during our vacations. I vividly remember one trip in particular. I was 5 years old, and my parents and I stood in the Philadelphia Zoo gawking at a very strange-looking animal. I noticed my mom and dad searching for the name placard on the animal's cage. I walked up to the rail and quite confidently told my parents that it was an okapi. They, of course, thought I was speaking gibberish until they saw the placard, – which read, "Okapi: *Although it bears striped markings reminiscent of the zebra, it is most closely related to the giraffe"*. Astonished, they asked me how I knew the name. I shrugged my shoulders and told them, "I just knew." At 5 years old, I had probably seen it on *Sesame Street*. The point being, I was already showing an aptitude and passion for animals.

Dogs came into my life at a very early age, as well. My grandparents always kept stray dogs that wandered into their garden. Their adoption list included Heinz 57's to purebreds, including one German Shepherd police dog. I remember as a little girl painting a ceramic figure of one of my grandmother's favorite strays, Dizzy. I still have that much-cherished figurine today.

At my grandparents' house, I began to feel a connection with dogs. The former police dog, King, hated almost everyone but me. I knew he trusted me; I did not fear him and was always calm around him. The adults were concerned about his temperament and wanted little to do with him, but they also saw how gentle he was with me. He let me sit with him and he even played ball with me. I never acted like an erratic child around him, which often happens with children. My calm demeanor began to show its value, especially in relation to acceptance by dogs.

I learned a good deal about life through these animals, too. One afternoon, I went to check on another of my grandparents' dogs, Cersee the bulldog. She was a stray female that had gotten pregnant by another stray dog. The animal warden knew my grandmother and brought her the dog to foster. I will never forget crying after I saw the blood around Cersee; I thought she chewed off her leg! I had no idea I just witnessed the birth of her single puppy. I also learned about death during this time, as Dizzy aged and developed complications from diabetes. He had to be put to sleep to prevent him from suffering any longer. When I arrived at my grandparents house the next morning, they told me what had happened and let me say goodbye to him before he was buried. These dogs had become part of the family to me, and it was a type of bond I would never forget.

The most memorable of all the dogs was the one my parents chose for us, Moses. He was an awesome dog. One of the cutest dogs I have ever seen, Moses was a multi-pedigreed dog – which meant he had lots of breeds in his DNA. His dad, Toby, was a beautiful Sheepdog and Standard Poodle mix, while his mother, Betsy, was this awful-looking Cocker Spaniel and Miniature Poodle mix. Both Toby and Betsy were great dogs in their own right.

The first night Moses was home with us, my dad fashioned a cardboard divide to keep him in a small area of the kitchen. The little den contained his food and water of course, and newspaper for his house training. Later that night, after everyone was asleep, Moses whined as a puppy often would in a new situation. Even the old "ticking alarm clock" trick did not work for the little pup. He still whined. Being a light sleeper, and after I heard him I quietly snuck downstairs and brought Moses up to my bedroom. My sister was still asleep in her bed, and I curled up in mine with the new "baby".

After a few minutes, I realized that the puppy was moving. He crawled out from under the covers and down to the bottom of the bed, where he wet all over my bed linens. Well, at 8 years old, not knowing what else to do, I pulled off the sheets and took him back downstairs to his den. Then I crawled in bed with my sister and went back to sleep. I did not realize at the time that I was behaving in line with our human nature to comfort and console. I had heard the puppy whine and I felt sorry for him, when in all actuality it was a potty visit that Moses needed. Even if that had not been the case, I had already started misinterpreting his language. I gave comfort at the wrong time – for a dog. There is definitely a right time, but I will explain more about this later in the book.

I don't remember details of the next day, but over the years Moses and my family grew very close. He bonded with my mother so much that to this day she has never had another dog. Stories of Moses still bring a tear to my mother's eyes. Moses lived a great, long life, and his memory and spirit are very strong. As I look back at his life, I wish I would have had my present knowledge and skills to help him have an even better life. I could have helped him through his fear of thunder storms, lightning, and fireworks. We all could have helped him if we only understood. He was a great little leader, and he did his best to look after us. We were lucky to get a dog with such a wonderful personality. Or were we lucky? Did we simply unknowingly attract the right dog into our family?

Well, as you know, you cannot dwell on the past, so I can only take these types of experiences and use them to shape who I want to become, and that has ultimately made me who I am today. Life is about learning and growing, and although I did not know it at the time, Moses helped me grow.

As time passed, many other animals entered my life, and I was able to have a special connection with many of them. Animals are at ease with me. People have watched in amazement as their temperamental cat curled up in my lap or their indifferent dog suddenly showed interest. This came as no surprise to me, however, because I always knew I wanted to work with animals. I received my degree in Psychology, with an emphasis on learning and behavior. I completed an internship at a zoo and became certified in large animal rescue. Some of my most memorable experiences are from rescuing animals from emergency situations while I worked as a professional firefighter.

For years I thought about writing a book, but it was not until my work with dogs that I knew what book I should write. I discovered my purpose in life and thus grew to understand a very powerful force. This force is one of the universal laws of nature called the Law of Attraction. I will explain more about these laws in the book. The moment I awoke with the idea for *From Wags to Riches* the events around me fell into place. I made the decision and did not think, "How can I possibly do this"? I never worried about the how; I just knew it would happen. I needed to relax and believe. I truly feel that if you believe, then you will succeed.

"Belief in oneself is one of the most important bricks in building any successful venture."
– Lydia M. Child

Even though I saw the bigger picture and a "successful venture", I was unaware that the events occurring in my day-to-day activities were leading me to fulfill my vision. My life had been a rollercoaster from some pretty low times to an age of enlightenment, which now has been very exciting and fun. I will share many of those times with you throughout the chapters to follow. There have been a few moments I strayed from the path, but eventually I found my way back. When a rocket is on its path to the moon, it strays off course most of the time. The ship is always correcting course to reach its target. The time spent in correcting is all it takes for a successful trip. This has been a similar path for my life, as well. My course is that of an educator and a rescuer by nature, and I believe the animals are helping me find my way.

With each animal I attract into my life, I am taught another lesson in personal growth. It never matters how small the animal is, they all have something to share. In turn, my goal is to teach you what I have learned. *From Wags to Riches* will offer you the insights into the sources of my learning – the animals in my life, especially the dogs. So as you look toward your journey, you too may be off course on occasion, but with the lessons learned you will hit your target.

INTRODUCTION

I thought I was simply helping out a friend…

My career as a professional firefighter was over because of an injury. Even though I was still living in Virginia, I was planning a move to Orlando, Florida. My family was located there, and I wanted to be closer to my nephews and parents. A month before moving , I agreed to take a Dalmatian named Spanner from a fellow firefighter. He was unable to keep the dog and did not know where to turn.

Spanner was an old dog that was set in his ways. He definitely had his share of problems, both behaviorally and physically. I did not really know what I was getting into, but it was a turning point for me. It was the beginning of a new path, and I had no idea at the time where it would lead. Little did I know how much this one dog would be responsible for teaching me, guiding me, and setting me on an incredible journey. I simply thought I was helping out a friend, yet I received much more out of the deal.

I learned some of Spanner's habits the first evening I fed him. I did not know that he was very resource aggressive, which means he did not want anyone near his stuff! I did not give myself enough space to move past him once his food was down. It took quite a bit of time until I was finally able to leave the room because his bed was also between me and the door, and that was more of "his stuff". It was a great learning experience, and I realized how nervous I was while I worked my way past him. I was definitely giving off the wrong feeling and "vibes", but these were things I had yet to understand. At that moment, all I knew was this dog was not happy with me being in his space, and I was not happy being there, either! I needed to learn quickly how to deal with this dog. I went to a co-worker who was experienced with search-and-rescue dogs to ask her advice. She explained I might be able to change Spanner's bad habits since he had not yet settled into his new place. So I worked with the old guy. I saw early on that it was going to be a battle of wills, so I just put his food down and moved away as not to appear a threat. I left him to eat alone and in peace. Later, I actually learned that my behavior around food was an important key in the dog's world.

The month went by and I moved to Florida. That was definitely a tough trip for the old dog. Since Spanner had hindquarter and knee issue it was not easy for him to lie down and settle on the floor, let alone in a moving truck. He growled anytime he was in the backseat, so it was always a thrill traveling with the "Cujo dog" behind me. It was a constant wonder whether I was going to lose an ear. He never did bite anyone, but he snapped at people quite often.

After living in Florida for only a few months, Spanner developed a serious problem. He had small cysts on his back, and every now and then one would erupt. The day he was supposed to visit the dermatologist, he could not walk. I carried him to the car and drove to Affiliated Veterinary Specialists (AVS). Luckily all the specialists were in this one facility, so Spanner went right in to the neurologist before seeing the dermatologist. After a battery of tests, nothing was confirmed. It appeared to be neurological, but without further expensive testing I would not know anything conclusive. I went home with antibiotics and steroids, and a skin culture was sent off to the lab. The doctors and staff at the facility were very helpful during this stressful time. They told me that if he couldn't walk in three days, then he would not walk again.

Spanner's story will be continued later in the book. He had lessons to teach us that I will share in the following chapters. During the time Spanner lived with me, other dogs found their way to me as well. I will also talk about them and the lessons they shared in greater detail throughout the book. When I first arrived in Florida, I started an animal sanctuary that was supposed to be a bird and reptile refuge. However, other animals in need seemed to find their way to me. Some of those animals came as strays, others as neglect or relinquishments. As times were changing, I had to change with them. I needed to consider a new mission. I will share the story behind that decision as you read on.

Circumstances in my life moved me toward a greater good without me knowing. It would be a few more years until my eyes were fully opened and I would understand it all. That is the thing about nature and the universe. It is orderly even when we do not see it. We must trust that situations are happening for a reason, and when we are ready, we will uncover the meaning.

This book is as much for you as it is for your dog. As we continue, I will show you just how important these creatures are to our human society. I will guide you to discovering the secrets to attracting success in life just by listening to your dog. It is my wish to pass this onto you to give you the insight you will need on your journey.

CHAPTER
–One–

Who is this Wolf in
Your Living Room?

CHAPTER
– One –

How many times have you come home to have your dog greet you with the excitement of a jumping bean? His tail wags uncontrollably as he follows your every step, bouncing up and down. Later that evening, as you sit and relax in your favorite fluffy chair, you look down to see him lying at your feet chewing up your favorite pair of slippers. Have you thought to yourself, "Just who is this creature I'm living with"? If you have, you are not alone. What many people may not even be aware of is just how important these "wolves" in our living room are. I will share how this "wolf" came to be here, but to do that we have to jump back in time. First, we need to start out with a few stories of how we humans may have benefited from our dogs' wild ancestors in ways you may find hard to believe.

WOLVES TEACHING HUMANS

According to Wolf Song of Alaska, a non-profit organization geared toward wolf conservation and education, ancient dogs probably taught early humans some essential tricks. Recent theorizing maintains that this may have been helpful to our actual survival thousands of years ago. The most recent research comes from Australia, where scientist Paul Tacon and bio-archaeology consultant Colin Pardoe have published growing evidence that the wolf-human relationship may go back over 100,000 years.

Some of their findings include that wolves could have offered early humans some lessons in cooperation. Non-human primates have good parenting skills, but same-sex groups are not typically found living harmoniously. The cooperation evident in wolf packs may have given humans the impetus to cooperate more among themselves. Tacon is says, "We believe there were several forces that led to the development of anatomically and behaviorally modern humans, and that the close relationship between our human ancestors and wolves was one of the key factors." So, those old dogs may have taught humans some new tricks!

Wolves and Human Families

There is an interesting feature of child-rearing in humans that is not found among chimpanzees, gorillas, and orangutans. All primates are social, but only humans exhibit a strong devotion and caring toward their young.

Our species does not seem hard-wired for this behavior, especially when you look to the mothers of the other ape groups. They collectively care for their young, while the fathers mainly defend the home territory, with an occasional struggle for domination. Where did our family structure come from? It is very possible that we took on a behavior model that was from a species becoming increasingly closer to our hearts.

Wolves are an excellent example. Even though you can find the lone wolf, wolves for the most part thrive and have the highest likelihood of survival in packs. These are simply extended family groups. Packs are usually defined by blood ties, but on occasion a lone wolf might get adopted by a pack, or find another lone wolf to start a family with. The hierarchical structures within packs start from the alpha couple, usually the parents, to the various betas, down to an omega and any pups that may have recently been born. Even with the hierarchy, the roles of individual wolves change over their life spans. Wolves display a group approach to family structure and family care. They share caretaker roles for the pups.

In addition to the survival benefits of packs, wolves share a sense of communal bonding and responsibilities. It is highly possible that humans may have acquired their family structures from wolves. These notions did not simply materialize; they had to have a source, and wolves represent one of the most equitable forms of society among wild species.

Let's move forward in time to when most scientists believe that domestication was beginning to take place.

About 12,000 years ago, in an area now known as Israel, a body was buried in a grave cradling a pup in its hand. A young canid and a young human had been buried together. No one knows whether it was a dog or a wolf. This young hunter-gatherer is one of the earliest pieces of fossil evidence of dog's domestication and may be a clue to the history of dogs. Humans at this point in history began to view these animals less as beasts and more as creatures with spiritual qualities, thus deserving a proper burial.

The domestication of the dog reaches back approximately 14,000 years, and there is much debate about how it actually happened. There are a couple of different theories on the subject. One is that humans took wolf pups, and as they grew, some were more inclined to stay with people. Thus, those traits were then passed on.

Another theory is that wolves domesticated themselves by adapting to a new environment. As human society grew, they began leaving larger amounts of leftover food on the ground. Wolves, like humans, come in an assortment of personality types. Some are naturally more timid. Such wolves would have stayed away from humans altogether. Wolves with a more inquisitive nature adapted better as the human population grew. These wolves benefited from the easily accessible food. The scavenging canids that were less likely to flee from people survived on humans' "leftovers", and as a result succeeding generations became increasingly tame.

As time went on in human development, we grew weaker in certain sensory modes, while our brains grew larger and more complex. As our sense of smell diminished, we may have grown to rely on those increasingly tame canids to help us hunt and alert us to danger. This would have been the beginning of a split between wolves living beside us and wolves living with us.

We Were Slowly Developing "Man's Best Friend"

Domestic dogs initially had a uniform appearance. They were wolf-like mongrels. The first breeds appeared about 5,000 years ago in ancient Egyptian artwork. They lacked the exaggerated traits associated with contemporary breeds. As civilization progressed, dogs evolved with the need to perform functions within the community. Some worked with livestock, while others were used as guards. Approximately 150 years ago, we began to deliberately use selective breeding of dogs to develop specific physical types that were considered ideal for each breed. Over 80 percent of the current breeds did not exist!

This selective breeding is the science of eugenics. It is the "perfection" of a species. During the Victorian Era and into the rise of the Industrial Revolution, people began to look for perfection. If you look at the architectural designs of the day, the gardens, even the livestock, you will see a desire for customization. Thus, in the 19th century, there was an explosion of dog breeds. Dog DNA is highly malleable. Scientists now know that wolves, coyotes, foxes, in fact all canids, have a special segment within their DNA that repeats. This allows for physical variations among the breeds. Other mammals do not have this diversity, and this is the key to our ability to selectively breed dogs.

In 1873, enthusiasts from England formed what we now know as the Kennel Club. As a result of this club, stud books set standards for certain dog breeds, and basic rules for shows were established. Soon after the formation of the Kennel Club, other countries followed suit forming similar organizations, such as the American Kennel Club and its Canadian counterpart.

Today, at least 460 different breeds span the world. Some breeds, such as the American Coonhound, remain localized to specific regions of a country. Other breeds, such as the German Shepherd dog, have become popular across the globe.

Despite the fact that the majority of breeds today have found their way into our living rooms as family pets, most were first used to perform specific tasks, such as herding, hunting, and guarding. Their temperament, physique, and behavior developed according to their tasks.

As culture and society changed, our need for the dog to do what it was bred to do decreased. A good example of this is the

Tibetan Spaniel. Monks bred these dogs as lapdogs to help keep their bodies warm. The role of the dog then shifted from a working one to that of a companion. Today's dog rarely has anything to do with its original genetic breeding.

Unfortunately, we now expect the dog to live according to our behavioral rules and forget that they are an entirely different species. We no longer let dogs be dogs, often to the detriment of man's best friend.

COMMUNICATING WITH CANINES

Have you seen dogs jump up to greet their owners, bark at strangers, or roll over when another dog approaches? Then you already know something about how wolves communicate. Dogs inherited their language from their ancestors, the wolves. When we think about communication, we consider only speaking or writing, for these are the main two ways we as humans share information. But what about wolves, how do they "converse"? Even though they do not have the ability to form words or write, wolves can communicate effectively in several ways. One of the techniques is through body language to convey the rules of the pack. A friendly submissive greeting has the ears flattened and lips pulled back. An aggressive challenge will start with a stare down. A playful wolf dances and bows. Do you remember seeing your puppy bow to its litter mates?

Wolves have a very good sense of smell, which is about 100 times greater than that of humans. They use this sense for communication in a variety of ways. Wolves mark their territories with a behavior called scent-marking. When wolves from outside of the pack smell these scents, they know that an area is already occupied. Dominant animals may scent mark through urination as often as every two minutes. Ever notice your dog lifting its leg on every tree down the block? Wolves use their sense of smell, not only to alert them to nearby food or enemies, but also to communicate as well. This type of communication is done through a chemical message sent between members of the same species. The chemicals are known as "pheromones".

What about a wolf's howl? They're not just howling to make noise, they are actually communicating. They don't just howl at night, they call any time of the day; but we mostly hear them in the evening when the wind dies down and they are most active. Have you ever joined in a good ol' howl session with your dogs when there were sirens in the distance that they could hear?

As dogs were going to enter my sanctuary, I thought I should learn more about raising and living with this species. At the bookstore I found a book by Jan Fennell. I selected this book because the foreword was written by Monty Roberts, the author of *The Man Who Listens To Horses*. I was a huge fan of his gentle horsemanship, even though I never had horses nor did I ride. I knew he was one of those special people with animals, and I wanted to learn all I could from him. When I read the foreword, I believed this was the book for me. If this man was endorsing Jan Fennell's *The Dog Listener* then I was going to listen to what she had to say.

Jan's book opened my eyes. If I was going to be working with dogs, then I should understand their language. If we do not understand a species, we will have a difficult time learning from it, let alone communicating with it. As I continue to explain the canine language, I can show you how important these creatures are to human society.

Some of the stories in this book revolve around people who follow the Jan Fennell method called Amichien Bonding. The word describes it best. From the French, we are friends to the dog. We give our friends what they need by understanding and speaking their language. We convey to dogs in simple ways to show them that we can be the decision-maker, the leader of the pack. What is important is that your dog is getting what they truly deserve-- a happy, relaxed, and stress-free life. This is the way to the ultimate relationship with your dog. The dog can give back to you tenfold, retaining their full spirit. The canine species is so amazing that even dogs that have owners who do not quite "speak" their language will still give special gifts of enlightenment, joy, fulfillment, and much more. As I share this next brief story, you will see the importance of understanding the "wolf" language as a key in gaining the bond that we all strive to achieve with our dogs.

REMEMBER THESE RULES

A recent *Men's Journal* article shared a story of a man moving into a new situation with new roommates. One of those mates was a very large canine. The roommate was told not to look the wolf-shepherd mix in the eyes, not to touch him, not to speak to him but also not to feel any fear. The wolf-dog was a rescue from an abusive situation and did not take kindly to strangers. If these rules were not followed, he was told there could be trouble.

One morning after the roommate returned home for lunch, he found the dog in its outdoor enclosure but with the water bowl overturned. The temperature was 101 degrees and it seemed cruel not to intervene. Carefully, he entered the enclosure with the dog keeping a close watch and issuing a low guttural growl. The man slowly filled the bowl. The dog's growls ended as he began to lap up the water.

Later that evening, the relationship seemed to have changed between the dog and the roommate. There were no longer any growls. Over time, their bond deepened and the roommate was able to scratch the wolf-dog's head and share some affection. They continued to grow closer into a friendly pair.

Their transition has mirrored the flow of dog-human evolution. The relationship between the species opened in deep enmity, moved toward tolerance, and only in the end blossomed into a deep bond. Humans and dogs now enhance each other's lives in many ways, from the purely pragmatic to the deeply emotional.

My mentor and dear friend, Jan Fennell, showed me how truly important communication is between us and our canines. As I began to work with Jan, I sensed her tremendous knowledge and ability with dogs, and I truly believed I had found something incredible. I still do to this day. Jan's method has really taken the canine language and human abilities and combined them to work perfectly to help our dogs. She has been able to teach people the canine language.

I also saw how this applies to our human-to-human relationships. If you truly want to communicate with not only dogs but humans as well, you must speak their language. Most people do not have a fulfilling relationship with their dogs simply because they are not speaking in a language the dog understands. Yes, you can use psychological conditioning to achieve some results with your dogs, but to break through and really communicate will bring you that deeper bond. People often expect the dog to understand our language even though we are supposed to be the species with greater intellect. If we use that intellect, we can actually communicate with them more effectively. Just think of computers – they have their own language, and if you don't understand or speak that language then you will not get the computer to do what you want. It works the same with dogs.

Jan learned to communicate with dogs by going back to the wolf to learn their language, a process that made perfect sense. Dogs and wolves have almost the same genetic makeup, with only a .02 percent difference in the DNA. Despite their virtual identical genetic makeup, there are differences between the two.

Wolves rarely bark. When they do, it is a quick muffled sound, usually when they are afraid or hurt. A dog bark is distinctively different than a wolf bark. Wolves also do not have a predisposition to such canine disorders as hip dysplasia or any other genetic disorders caused by poor breeding. In the United States alone, one out of every four purebreds has some genetic problem. Wolves and dogs differ in some physical characteristics, but the hormonal differences cause the most profound effects in behavior between them. These differences cause the dog to never behave like a fully matured canine. A dog stays in an arrested developmental stage; they act like adolescent wolves their whole lives. They are far less territorial and predatory. This makes them great companions to humans.

Jan learned what mattered most to wolves, and she also saw how they interacted to form a highly cohesive pack unit. The areas of survival were of key importance. These are: when the pack goes on a hunt; when the pack eats; when the pack is in danger; and when the pack reunites after a separation. I will go into this more in a later chapter, but this next story is a great example of how Jan came to understand canine language. Pat Wright recounts the experience she shared with Jan.

Yellowstone Adventures

While on a wolf/bear expedition in Yellowstone Park, I witnessed an amazing event with Jan Fennell, "The Dog Listener" of England. Jan and I had been in the park for five days or so and our sightings of wolves in action had been very minimal, which is expected in Yellowstone.

You see, wolves are very shy, quiet creatures. They are not the aggressive killer that many fairy tales and humans would lead you to believe. They would rather risk their life attempting to take down a 2,000 pound elk or buffalo than get anywhere near a human being. A sighting is rare and a privilege. Just why humans are hell-bent on shooting them is something I cannot understand. They are the top of the food chain in their natural environment and keep the ecosystem in balance.

Early one morning, my Yellowstone guide, Linda, alerted us to a wolf sighting in the Lamar Valley. Having heard of sightings here and there, we set up our field scopes in different places only to hear of another place. We rushed to break down the equipment and took off to the next sight. Then, we got another call that sounded really good, so we went through the procedure of breaking down the equipment again and rushing to yet another sight. Once there, we were pleasantly surprised that wolves were present, only visible through the scope. They were probably a mile or more away. They were bedded down under the shade of a tree in the sagebrush. You could see a head pop up to see what was going on.

We noticed a young elk drifting toward the wolves, unaware of their presence. Suddenly, the elk realized that it had come too close to its most feared enemy. Its ears went flat and it froze. The wolves saw the opportunity. As fast as lightning, two wolves jumped up and began the chase. The elk burst away desperately to get back to its herd, which it was able to do. At this point, the other four wolves joined in the chase.

32

Beautiful black wolves darted in and out of the sagebrush chasing the elk to get them to run to look for a weakness. When it was clear to the alpha male that there were no weak elk in the herd, he simply stopped and walked up the hill to the high ridge. He never looked back once.

Once he got to the top of the ridge, he stood very still. By this time, the other wolves had caught up to him and were somewhat agitated. One by one, they went up to the alpha male with their tail tucked under them. They walked low to the ground and licked the face of the alpha male. They were asking the alpha if he was still in charge, "Were you injured while on the hunt?" The alpha male answered by looking away every time a wolf licked his face as if to say, "I am fine and still in charge, so stay out of my space." Once the fifth wolf had done this and gotten the answer that he was looking for, all of the tails came up and wagged. The stress of possibly losing the leader was gone and every wolf was clearly happy. The alpha male was still able to hold the position. Once the decision had been made that the original pack hierarchy was still intact, the alpha male walked up the ridge with the rest of the pack following in single order behind him. They quietly and calmly just disappeared behind the ridge.

WOW! This was decision-making and reuniting at its finest. It can't get much better than that.

Pat Wright Willington, Connecticut
www.baywoodkennels.com

Obviously, we cannot growl, howl, or posture like a wolf to communicate with our dogs, but we can use very specific areas to prove ourselves capable of giving a dog what they need. This holistic method of working all four of these elements into life with our dogs on a day-to-day basis will allow us to convey to our dogs that we are responsible for them. When they see these signals from you, they know you are in charge. Knowing this will allow the dog to become stress free. You are now "speaking" the same language.

This next story on partnership is a great example of growing together with the pack's relationship. The writer, Nancy Fishinger, has a wide variety of knowledge of different dog "training" methods and she understands canine language as well. There is no need to be a bully to have a great working relationship with your pack.

PARTNERSHIP!

I have lived with dogs all my life. Dogs have lived with me all of my life. Which is it?

What I have come to realize is not the true picture. Dogs and I have formed a partnership! Growing up, the first was the case. My mother always said that our dogs let us live with them. She was just kidding, but to a certain extent this was true. Though we lived with them, you might say that they were in charge. During that time, we had between one and three dogs, and while not an overwhelming situation, I know in retrospect that I was not the leader – so one of them had to be.

Sometime following college ,my life took a decided turn when a small Toy Fox Terrier by the name of Elvis came along. It quickly became apparent that some training would be necessary, so Elvis and I enrolled in an obedience class. Our trainer, Claire Koshar, explained that she felt "Terriers are born with more original sin" than other groups of dogs.

During this phase of my life, I became very involved with competition in dog shows, both obedience and conformation. There was a great deal of training and travel. Additionally, I had become a Toy Fox

Terrier breeder and a United Kennel Club judge. A second breed, the Chinook, became a part of my life.

At this time, life became very structured and I had become the leader – or so I thought. The dogs did "live with me" and together we got a lot done.

I was doing a good deal of "teaching", which meant imparting knowledge to somebody. Now, I know that just because I was instructing my dogs in the skills of sits, downs, recalls, and gaiting in the ring, it did not mean that I had taken the job of "leader" off of my dogs.

Currently, dogs are still, and always will be, a vital part of my life. The difference is having formed, what I like to call, a partnership. The dogs and I are now learning from each other daily. That is correct, I said, learning. About a year ago, I attended a class given by Jan Fennell, the Dog Listener. During the course, I learned about Amichien Bonding and establishing "Leadership of the Pack." Along with my classmates, I was introduced to the four key elements of bonding: reuniting, danger signals, taking charge of the walk, and food power.

As I began putting these elements into practice, the first challenge was to not complicate what was simple. My mission was to let the dogs in my pack pick me as their leader – letting it be their decision. But I would need to do the things required for them to make that decision. At the onset, I have to admit, I was a bit stressed with facing the true responsibilities of being the "leader of the pack". Very quickly, I saw a change taking place. One by one, individual dogs became more relaxed. With that I was more relaxed. Before you knew it, we were bonding in a new way. I was the leader, and we were all very happy and comfortable. Ours was a partnership that would stand the test of time.

Our pack has recently lost one of its members. Victor, our 17-year-old rescue Toy Fox Terrier, crossed over the "rainbow bridge" and will be missed by all.

He was the ancient and wise one – even when he was 2 years old! As our pack adjustings to our loss, we will also be accepting in a 9-week-old Chinook puppy. We have lost an old soul and have gained a young soul. The pack will survive – that is what packs do. That is what families do throughout the world. In closing, I would like to quote two of my dog buddies and mentors.

"Be good to your dogs!"
– Claire Koshar, owner of 3J Dog Training School

"Don't complicate simplicity!"
– Jan Fennell, author of *The Dog Listener*

Nancy Fishinger, Montverde, Florida
Pippa Passes Hollow Kennels

Nancy & two of her Chinooks

Working with dogs as Nancy does, in "partnership", is a great way to open ourselves to the lessons the dogs can teach us.

There are many methods of training out there and many different philosophies. Some are very harsh, while others are positively oriented. But if only one party is getting what they want or the other party is in a state of stress, that does not sound like a party I want to attend. Whatever method you use, look into your dog's eyes. Really look into them. Are they soft and relaxed or do they show anxiety? Do they have that "wide-eyed" look? Do you have to resort to the use of prong collars or shock collars? Does your dog pant all the time, or pace and follow you everywhere as you move? If he does, then he is not relaxed.

Communicating with your dog is important for both of you. No matter if it is with humans or dogs, you must be able to communicate in order to have an effective relationship. This effective relationship is the key to the dog giving back to you , and for you to start on your journey of discovery.

As I learned Jan's method and implemented it into my relationships with my own dogs, I began to have a much nicer, calmer, more relaxed atmosphere around my dogs. This did not happen overnight, but there were immediate improvements in many areas, including in my personal life, as well. One very important thing I learned from this method and my life with the dogs is that to give is much better than to receive, and when you do that wholeheartedly, you actually get back monumental rewards.

"The most important thing in any relationship is not what you get but what you give.... In any case, the giving of love is an education in itself."
– Eleanor Roosevelt

I have actually lived it and seen it unfold between my dogs and me. When you give dogs the right kind of love and guidance, the education they give back to you is amazing. This is when you will be able to improve your life in any area you choose.

"We should give as we would receive, cheerfully, quickly, and without hesitation; for there is no grace in a benefit that sticks to the fingers."
– Roman Statesman Seneca

I give this information to you, cheerfully, quickly, and without hesitation. My goal is to help any dog owner achieve the ultimate relationship with their dog. I also want to see these same owners realize a greater fulfillment in their personal lives. They then can help other dogs and owners, and together we can work toward giving back our canine friends the joy of being a dog. The joy comes from being a relaxed and happy dog without any concern or fear. The return you get will be even greater.

As we continue into the next chapter, I will help you to understand the universal laws of nature that guide each and every one of us whether we know it or not. I will show you just how important our dogs are to us. After all, the evolution of the canine's habitat has gone from the wild to the barnyard, to the front yard, the front porch, the living room, the bedroom, onto the bed, and now many are even under the sheets!

CHAPTER
– Two –

The Nature of the Beast
Within Us All

CHAPTER
–*Two* –

You may have heard about the laws of the universe in relation to your own life. If not, learning about these laws is the first step in creating the ultimate relationship with your dog. In this chapter, I will attempt to answer the question: What are these laws and how do they relate to your dog?

Dogs guide us through life and teach us just how important the universal laws really are. Learning these laws allows us to fulfill our dogs' needs more easily and will help us grow in understanding. We are able to accept what comes into our lives, because we acquire the knowledge to understand what has happened. We learn to bring into our lives what we want, because we now have clearer insights into how the universe works. It is all about vibrations. You know, "good vibes". It is also about cause and effect, rhythm, polarity, relativity, gender, and energy. Nature has the answers. And our dogs are closer to nature and better able to act as our guides. They are the perfect go-between for keeping us rooted and helping us grow.

"By loving and understanding animals, perhaps we humans shall come to understand each other."
– Dr. Louis J. Camuti

In The Early Days

Dogs guided us in the early years of our development as seen in the stories from Chapter 1. Our behaviors in today's society, however, have caused the dogs to be stressed out, nervous, aggressive, and to have all sorts of behavioral problems. The number of dogs needlessly euthanized each year is astronomical. Not only are we not benefiting from our domesticated charges, but we are also creating problems for their species beyond what it has ever experienced before.

"Develop an 'attitude of gratitude.' Say thank you to everyone you meet for everything they do for you."
– Brian Tracy

It is always important to remember to appreciate what or who is in our lives and think about why they are there. It is wise to develop and maintain an attitude of gratitude for what is around us. This ensures a good feeling to bring the life we want not only with our dogs, but with our family, friends, and career as well.

This process of gratitude is the first step to changing your thinking and your energy toward the positive. Start to be grateful for all the things in and around your life. If we concentrate on what we are grateful for, we will not have room to focus on the problems or the complaints. Today's society is great at focusing on the negative. Simply pick up a newspaper, turn on the TV, or read some book reviews. It is okay to be aware of what is going on, but it is more important to be conscious of the great things and people around you. In Wallace Wattle's book, *The Science of Getting Rich,* the chapter on gratitude is a very important one. He wrote, "The daily practice of gratitude is one of the conduits by which your wealth will come to you." His definition of wealth does not only include money but all the good things you want in your life.

It is impossible to bring more into our lives when we are feeling ungrateful for what we have. Those feelings of ungratefulness are negative. We want to stay in a positive vibration. A good way to start is to show gratitude for your canine companions. Write down what you're grateful for and read it daily. Do not feel silly; this is a very important step. You can keep it private, but go ahead and do it. Start out saying how happy and grateful you are for _____. Maybe it is the unconditional love they show you, or their "happy to see you" tail wags. Maybe you just appreciate their company or being there to listen when no one else is. Whatever it is, you are grateful for, write it down, read it every day, and really feel it. The feelings are very important. So truly feel what you are saying, do not just read the words. Write down the other things in your life you are grateful, for as well. If we start our day reading and feeling grateful we will start to develop the good vibes that begin to make our lives all we want. It is all part of the same process to develop that attitude of gratitude. Make it a habit and change the vibrations, and you will be ready for the next step.

Since dogs are closer to nature, in many ways they have been and continue to be our guides to an improved life. Let us take a closer look at these universal laws.

The universal laws are all inter-related and are founded on the understanding that everything in the universe is energy. Everything that exists - whether it be nature, sound, color, oxygen, the wind, thoughts, emotions, your house, your physical body, your dog, everything you can see, hear, smell, and imagine - is a manifestation of this energy. Our own bodies are composed of atoms that vibrate rapidly. All of our thoughts, feelings, words, and actions are forms of energy. Everything we think, feel, say, and do in each moment can come back to us to create our realities. Have you ever heard the phrase, "What goes around, comes around"? That statement is very true because energy moves in a circle. Understanding the universal laws helps us learn to control our thoughts and emotions. Our animals are guided by the very same universal laws, but they are much more connected and in touch with nature than we are. As we develop, we seem to lose sight of where we came from. We are so busy going through the motions of life that we tend to forget that important part of ourselves.

Before we go any further, let's take a moment and define each one of the universal laws.

THE LAW OF VIBRATION

Everything in the universe is in a constant state of motion. Each sound, thing, and thought has its own frequency – a vibration. Just as a pebble thrown into the water creates vibrations that appear as ripples traveling outward, your thoughts create vibrations that travel outward into the universe, and attract similar vibrations that become the circumstances in your life. The law of vibration exists and is always present. We are creating the conditions in our lives, whether we want to believe it to be true or choose to deny it. A good example of this vibration is a dog whistle. Although as humans we are unable to hear the sound that comes from it, there is no doubt that it releases a noise that man's best friend can clearly hear. That frequency is a vibration. Again, the rate of vibration is beyond our human capacity to sense and experience, but it surely exists.

The Law of Attraction is a subset of the Law of Vibration. Our thoughts, feelings, words, and actions produce energies which, in turn, attract "like" energies. Negative energies attract negative energies and positive energies attract positive energies. Things that vibrate with similar frequencies attract one another. The Law of Attraction is how we most often see things brought into our physical world. Action is required to bring about or "create" things on earth. We must engage in actions that support our thoughts, dreams, emotions, and words.

THE LAW OF CAUSE AND EFFECT

Every action has a reaction or consequence. It is a process that determines and produces the results that we experience in our lives on a day-to-day basis. The Law of Cause and Effect is at work everywhere, always, and in anything and everything. A thought, just like a seed, can only produce an outcome in relation to the seed that is planted. If your thought seed consists of fearful, anxious, and doubtful results, we now know that, through the Law of Attraction, those thoughts can only grow into and produce what is in relation to the seed planted; and you will receive fearful, anxious, and doubtful results. Nothing in your life happens by accident. When you succeed, there is a specific cause for your success.

THE LAW OF POLARITY

Everything is on a continuum and has an opposite. For every positive there is a negative. If what you perceive as bad did not exist, would you know when you were having a good experience? If poverty did not exist, would you know what it was like to experience wealth? If failure did not exist, would you know what it was to experience success? If there were no such thing as death, we could not fully enjoy and appreciate what it means to experience life.

Know that every challenge we face contains the seeds for the opposite as well. Success and failure are both present. This is what makes life a constant learning experience and great adventure.

Law of Gender

Every seed has a gestation or incubation period. The implication is everything that appears new is actually the result of things that already exisited but are now changing form. Therefore, nothing is ever created or destroyed. It simply changes form in the way an acorn grows into an oak tree. Your goals of what you want in life are already out there but in a different form. If you are "tuned in" to the right frequency, you can hear the "music of your life". Basically, this means that you receive what you want. The key with the Law of Gender is there is a gestation period and you may not know how long that is. Plant the seed, take the proper action, believe, and have faith in what you want, and then wait.

The Law of Perpetual Transmutation of Energy

Wow, what a mouthful, but it is an important universal law. Energy is always moving and eventually moves into physical form. It never stands still. Everything we see, hear, taste, touch, or smell is in a constant state of change. Every cell in your body is replaced in less than a year. You have changed and are not the same physical person you were last year. Thoughts are energy. Energy moves into physical form when enough thought is given to it. What are you imagining? What are you worrying about? What are you giving energy to? The image you hold in your mind most often materializes as results in your life.

The Law of Rhythm

Everything vibrates and moves to certain rhythms. These rhythms set seasons, cycles, and patterns. Each cycle reflects the regularity of the universe. The seasons come and go, like a pendulum. Our mood levels and awareness swing back and forth. After working hard on a project, your body needs to rest. We sleep, and then wake up. This law is applicable when you have a gut feeling about whether it is a good time to act or if you should wait. Later in the book, you will read the story of Oprah Winfrey and one of her dogs. See if you can find the Law of Rhythm in that story.

The Law of Relativity

Everything in our physical world is only made real by its relationship to something else. What is cold? For example, have you ever experienced frozen fingers after a snowball fight in the winter and then come inside to warm them up? When you run cold water over your hands, it feels warm in comparison to how cold your hands are. Likewise, if you feel you are not making enough money, how does that compare to someone in a third-world country? It is all relative. Events and objects in life "just are" unless we compare them to something else. Nothing in life has any intrinsic meaning, except the meaning we give it. Relationships are everything, and everything is due to relationships.

Here is a good example of putting it all together. Think about what you want and feel good about it. Stay focused on your vision and go with the flow instead of resisting it. If your dog is pulling on the lead and you try to pull against it, then you are out of rhythm. It can cause you frustration, and the effect is negative vibrations. Those negative feelings go right down the leash to your dog, and you lose any respect the dog might have for you. Instead, keep your goal of a loose leash in your mind. Take a deep breath when the dog pulls, feel good about being outside with your dogs, and focus on the positive that you are working with your best friend. Now go with the flow, and when he pulls simply change direction, use the circularness of energy. Keep moving in different directions, and soon he will start looking to you for the direction to go. With time and practice, the dog will no longer pull on the leash. This is a simplified example, but it is exactly how the universal laws work together with what your dog needs from you. It takes practice, but you will get plenty of opportunity, and; dogs are very willing but also forgiving teachers.

The Law of Attraction and Relationships

Frederick Buechner once wrote, "Your life and my life flow into each other as wave flows into wave, and unless there is peace and joy and freedom for you, there can be no real peace or joy or freedom for me". When we relate this quote to the universal laws and our relationship with our dogs, we can understand that we are all interconnected. If you treat your dog with harsh, commanding ways, then that same vibration will flow back to you in areas of your life that you may not even realize are connected. The next story will show the opposite of that. It's a story of one man putting peace and kindness out to the universe and what he got in return.

Great Neighbors

You could not ask to live next to better folks. Jimmy and Julie Bean are as good as they come. There is nothing that this man would not do to help someone. He has every tool anyone could ever need and always has a nice, cold beer waiting after a hot day in the Florida sun. He asks for nothing in return and is just a downright good guy. Julie is the best Southern cook I have ever met, and the gatherings at their home are wonderful. It is easy to see how such good folks attracted such a good dog.

Dromara's Sweet Gracie is a beautiful Golden Retriever from good bloodlines and champion parents from Maryland. Jimmy never wanted a show dog; he only wanted a healthy dog to be his companion. Not too long before this, he had lost his companion, Casey, and missed having a sidekick. Gracie came along and brought back a shine in Jimmy's eye. She is his good puppy, and he loved her the moment he met her. Gracie is a very smart dog and only needs gentle guidance. She is a dog that will do anything for people. She brings Jimmy his newspaper every morning. She would make a great therapy dog, because she loves being petted and lying next to someone. Gracie is happy to just be around everyone and loves to give a tail wag. She wants to give love and be there for people and wants nothing in return.

What Jimmy attracted in this situation is what he projected to the universe. Good vibrations and feelings at the right time brought him the type of dog that would suit his personality. This is just a simple example of how important our feelings are in what we attract. Think back to times when you attracted something you did not want or did not fit with you. What was going on with you around that time? Were you happy and feeling good, or did you have strife in your life? Without preparation, understanding, and practice, we can often attract things into our lives that we do not really want. Of course, things will also come into our lives to test us, but you will know the difference by how you are feeling.

Jimmy focused on exactly what he wanted, and he knew he would have it. He was never impatient about it or worried that he would not find the right dog. Jimmy was able to bring exactly what he wanted into his life, and now Sweet Gracie has a daddy who loves her very much.

Sweet Gracie

You attract others into your life whether you know it or not. We do this every day. Remember in my earlier story of Moses, when I asked if we were just lucky or did we somehow attract him to our family? That story showed several of the laws at work. The Law of Attraction/Vibration brought him into our lives. The Law of Gender showed I was not ready for the path I would take in understanding canine language. The laws of nature are always working. Unfortunately, we do not always attract what we want in our lives. When we understand the laws, we can begin to see how we are attracting what we are. Have you ever ended one relationship to simply start another that follows the same pattern? It is because of your internal feelings. Those need to change first, and then who you attract will change as well.

This does not mean that you are a bad person; it only means you are not in the right vibrational state for certain dog's needs. We may not completely understand this at times. Often, someone gets a dog or a dog finds them that seems completely incompatible to them. This may very well be the case, but you may have attracted the situation because of vibrations that you had been feeling. You may not have even been aware of it. People often say that opposites attract, but this is not the case. Nature strives to be in harmony. So when it seems that a shy person has attracted an outgoing person, or an active dog has found his way to a sedentary guy, what you actually have are two entities that have the same vibrational signals.

Remember, we attract everything into our lives. It is just a matter of attracting the right things and accepting whatever has been attracted to learn from it. This next story will show why it is so important to not question what you have attracted. Ellen, my partner at the rescue, and I will share how we learned that lesson the hard way.

PHOENIX'S STORY

The call came in from Kim while I was at work. I gave whatever time I could to helping the rescue, and she asked if I would be available that evening while she was out. The people at her doctor's office had found a stray puppy and, knowing she ran the animal rescue, contacted her. They needed to get the dog out of their facility, and animal control could not get there in a timely manner. So, off Kim went to take the pup and transfer her to the Humane Society. You see, her rescue was originally for birds and reptiles, not dogs. Kim brought the dog to her rescue until she could make her way to the shelter. The first time I saw this little doe-eyed pup was in the back-yard. She was maybe 6 months old, a small Pit Bull, brown with a white chest. Just wanting to please, she ran to each of us as we called her. She had some mange on her face and chest.

However, sweet as she was, we listened to what other people said, "You can't save them all", so Kim reluctantly took her to the Orange County dog pound. She made sure to leave her name as a last resort. A few days had passed and I could not get the pup out of my head. I stopped by the pound to check on her and she looked horrible. Her poor feet and face were terribly swollen, and I almost did not recognize her. I called Kim immediately to ask her what to do. Due to some bureaucratic procedures, I could not get the dog out right away. When I was finally able to bring her home, I took her straight to a vet. He sent me home with some medicine for her mange and mentioned that she might have Parvo but did not talk about treatment. At that time, neither Kim nor I had any experience with this deadly disease. Kim was just getting used to dealing with the old man Spanner and living in a new state when Phoenix showed up.

The pup suffered through the weekend, and I spent as much time as possible just sitting with her. We did not know how sick she was because she masked it so well. I just enjoyed cuddling with her. She had worsened very quickly as her little system was losing the battle against the virus. Kim took her to the vet on Tuesday, which was just four days since I pulled her from the pound. The vet was in a rush, and I just made it there before they put the needle in to put her down. It was confirmed that she had the Parvo virus.

Sometimes it feels like we learn such valuable lessons at the expense of the very sweetest lives. We both learned what Parvo is, a horrible virus that kills — sometimes quickly, sometimes painfully slowly, but always horribly. I called the pound about the Parvo afterward, since we determined, due to the timeframe, that she had contracted the disease while in their facility. All they had to say was that they knew they had a problem. So, we learned to never take a dog to the pound; we risk exposing them to all the diseases there.

We learned how hard it is to find a decent vet, not one bent on puting a dog down before it cuts into the lunch hour. I still feel responsible for her getting sick and losing her, and take full responsibility, as does Kim for the situation, but it was due to ignorance. So, we learned to educate ourselves and listen to our feelings. I understand now how important feelings are and to really let them be your guide. I now know that Kim is very good at attracting animals and people in need. She has that ability to help them, and for dear little Phoenix we did not recognize that in time. Out of the pain of losing her, we learned these vital lessons.

We focused too much on what others said and what others expected. I completely know now just how strong a force of nature the Law of Attraction is, as well as how the vibrations we give off can lead to success or failure. Animals and people come into our lives like the poem says, for a reason, a season or a lifetime. There is a definite reason to learn from this little girl. Nature can be cruel but these are the forces we live with, and if we do our best to understand them, we can make the best of this world and bring ourselves to a higher place. I do hope that, whatever had happened in her short life, the last couple of days she spent with me were better than some of the earlier days she had.

Ellen, Orlando, Florida
www.inharmonywithnature.org

The story of Phoenix is an example of (A) Understanding how the laws of nature work in our lives. The Law of Attraction, Cause and Effect, Polarity, Gender, and Transmutation of Energy all were at work. Can you see them? (B) Recognizing when it is at work by the results that come to us, and (C) correcting our path in the direction we want to go. In the stories throughout the book, you can find the laws at work. It is not so important to see it but rather that you know and understand them so you can understand why and how things are happening in your life and with your dog as well.

In my experience as a Dog Listener, I have come to understand the universal laws as extremely powerful forces that effect our lives. It does not matter whether we are aware of how these laws are working at any one time, be it with our animals or other humans. Simply put, what we give our focus, emotion, and attention to we attract into our lives. This is evident in our interactions with our dogs. Stop for a moment and think about how you interact with your dog. If you are in a positive frame of mind and relate to him with that same positive energy coupled with the right actions, your results will be better, because you are attracting positive vibrations. Likewise, if you are giving off negative vibrations, even with the correct actions, your results will be negative as well.

Now apply that to the rest of your life. You attract into your life what you think about – whether it involves your dog, career, family, or finances. Moving toward deliberate attraction (creating what you want) requires an awareness of our intention, attention and emotional state. Basically, we move from subconsciously creating events in our lives to consciously and deliberately affecting our experiences. You no longer need to be an extra in the movie of your life.

"If you don't program yourself, life will program you!"
– Les Brown

Think of yourself as a magnet. As a magnet, you attract, by way of your thoughts. Like attracts like. You become what you think about most and you attract what you think about most. Thoughts become things.

So, if we are thinking about all the things our dogs are doing wrong and those thoughts remain the object of our focus, then we will get more of the wrong things from our dogs. Start to focus on what we want from our dogs, be grateful for them, and take the proper action, then we will get what we want. Great dogs!

The Law of Attraction is helpful in teaching an awareness of our emotions and how they are affecting our experiences. It is of utmost importance to change our vibration, our feeling, if we are not happy with our dog, our family, our career, or our life. Our dogs will tell us if we are in a good vibration anyway. We can see it in their eyes and in how they act toward us. If you sound happy but internally are frustrated and angry, then your dog is not going to respond as willingly and energetically as if you have the right vibrations.

Now, you have a basic understanding of how the Law of Attraction brings you every event, condition, and circumstance that you experience. This occurs by a combination of thoughts, beliefs, and emotions all working together to create the results we see in our physical world. Now, you will understand and appreciate the next story even more.

Our Boy Bubba

His proper name was Brut. Named after the dry champagne, he seemed more like a bubba dog so his nickname became Bubba. A yellow Labrador Retriever with a funny sense of humor, Bubba used to get a kick out of startling people and letting them think he was a killer- attack dog. If Bubba was in the car or behind any glass, he would lay low on the seat or floor until some unsuspecting passerby walked close enough. At that point, he leapt up and barked ferociously and snarled at the window. His teeth gnashed at the glass, and saliva would fly everywhere. He even did this to the people that he knew and loved. As soon as they moved on, he ducked down to await his next victim. It was a sight to watch, and the more you jumped and acted startled, the better he liked it.

Boy, did Bubba have quirks! I understand them all now, but did not at that time. The first time I went to meet Bubba I was told it would be an experience. My new roommate, Edith, invited Bubba and her family over for a visit. I had recently moved into a townhouse in the Springfield, Virginia, area. I was working when Edith's family arrived with Bubba. As the day progressed, they decided to do some shopping. Well, this meant that when I arrived home, no one would be there, but the dog. Edith knew about my ability with animals and figured it would be fine. Her parents, however, were not so sure. They knew Bubba, or so they thought, and they worried about the meeting. They alerted me to the snarling that he would do through the glass, and they told me he really would not hurt anyone. All I needed to do was walk right in.

I felt completely confident as I went home to meet this guy. When I walked up to the front porch, Bubba snarled and gnashed at the glass, just as I expected. I kept my confidence, though, because I trusted my friend's knowledge of the dog. I continued to the front door and concentrated on opening it. What happened next was just something for the books. I walked in and said, "Hello, you must be Bubba". At that point, Mr. B turned tail and hid under the dining room table. Well, I just had to laugh. This most ferocious of dogs was a real scaredy cat.

I went in and carried on my business and then looked at Bubba, still under the table, and offered him a treat. Tentatively, he came out and snatched it from me, still unsure. When I addressed him once again, "It really was nice to meet you, Bubba", he scurried under the table to his safe spot. Again I laughed and waited until Edith and her family came home.

When they arrived and entered the house, I was watching TV, with Bubba hidden under the table. He ran out to greet them and looked relieved to see familiar faces, his tail wagging excitedly. They asked what happened and when I explained how he hid, they laughed. They assumed Bubba did not know how I knew his name since he did not know me. He was used to having the upper hand,

and with me he didn't. Bubba was content with me now that they were home. Later, he became very happy to greet me with his wagging tail.

Over the years, I grew quite fond of Edith's family and was invited to visit with them in their home. Mr. B, as he was often called, grew quite close to me and I grew to love the guy. His antics are enough to fill a book all on their own. Bubba was a wonderful character that truly took on the decision-making lead role with his pack. He was one of the lucky ones who managed to skirt real problems by the hair of his teeth. Bubba hated postal carriers and was not very good around children. He did not like other dogs and look out if you were a cat. However, when he first met my cat, it was a different story.

Spats did not live with me when I first moved in with Edith. He joined the household about two years later. This was a cat that never took anything from any dog! He was very sweet but stood his ground against the rival species. Spatty wandered around the house eager to see who was coming to visit. That was when Bubba made it into the house. Spats took one look at the dog and just waited. When Bubba made his charge up to Spats, the cat ran around the table with the dog following. Then the cat turned and gave him one good swat on the nose. Bubba ran and hid under the table and he never chased *that* cat again.

For all of Bubba's antics, he really was a dog who could have benefited from some better canine communication skills. Unfortunately, none of us knew them at the time. Looking back, I understand how we must have looked in Mr. B's eyes. We needed looking after, and he was going to do it. He was not very certain about our world, but if he questioned it, then the answer was to intimidate it and hope it went away. I have no doubt that Bubba would have been much more at ease with the right signals, but learning is a part of every life. Bubba passed away with cancer at the great age of 13. He was loved more than most dogs, and he had the most wonderful parents, who miss him dearly. I am still close to Edith and her parents, Edee and Ben; they are like family to me. Part of Bubba's legacy is his antics and those antics are the stuff that makes great memories of a great dog.

The Law of Attraction is always at work in and around us. The antics of Bubba followed in line with that because we added fuel to the fire, so to speak. There was always the concern for what Bubba was going to do in a particular situation. There was tension about taking him out in public around the possibility of other dogs. We all "expected" something from Bubba and he always delivered. You have already learned that you attract what you project. This is just the first of many examples about how the Law of Attraction is subtle yet huge in our own lives and in the lives of our dogs. Let's take the next step toward controlling what we get.

CREATIVE VISUALIZATION

Visualization, when combined with positive affirmation, is an extremely powerful technique in reprogramming the subconscious mind. The subconscious mind holds people back in life. I will use the word paradigm when I refer to your "way of thinking". You may hold a paradigm that "money cannot buy you happiness". If that is how you feel, then you are correct. If you want to change the results you get, you have to change your paradigm.

These paradigms control not only how we think but how we act, including how we act toward our dogs. If you have grown up witnessing dogs treated a certain way, or watching women treated a certain way, that behavior will follow you into your adult life. Is it the right way? From one perspective it may be correct, but from another it may be counterproductive. It is very important to look at it from the dog's perspective! Especially since your behavior affects them the most.

Although you may not be consciously aware of it, you are actually creating your current results based on those subconscious beliefs. Many people are not even aware that their previously held beliefs and subconscious programming are creating the conditions in their lives. They do not know that they actually have control over them! The majority believe that they have no control over many aspects of their lives. They believe that in the areas concerning money, health, and relationships there is nothing that could possibly change the situations they find themselves in everyday. These previously established beliefs could not be further from the truth.

There are ways to change those paradigms. We can reprogram our subconscious beliefs. Visualization is a way to do that. People visualize in different ways. No one way is better; it is just what works for you. Auditory awareness, visual awareness, and kinesthetic awareness are three ways to visualize. Focus on something you want to happen to see which way you best visualize. The first type is auditory awareness. The auditory types visualize with words and sounds or are more apt to hear the results of their visualization.

The second is visual awareness. This type of person actually sees the pictures or images in his mind. People who use visual awareness can clearly see the result of their visualization in great detail, much like on a movie screen. The third type is the kinesthetic. These people are more prone to the emotion, or feeling the results, during visualization. They can actually feel what it will be like to have their visualizations created. Remember, it is extremely important to visualize in a way that allows you to "feel" what it is like to "already have" whatever it is that you want.

We always want to visualize with the end result in mind. We do not want to focus on the things that we **do not want**. By allowing the problem into our awareness, we are actually nurturing it, giving it additional energy, and allowing it to grow. Along with the visualization, write out your desired outcome in detail and consistently review it, believe it has already happened and think about how good it is!

You have only good to gain by believing in what I have discussed with you in this chapter, so go ahead and incorporate it into your life. Whether you believe in the Law of Attraction or not, think of the words of a great man named Bob Proctor, "Just do it till you find out I'm lying or it doesn't work." As we proceed we are going to get into the core information of the book. These next chapters will show how dogs actually assist us with the skills necessary to have everything we want in life.

CHAPTER
–Three –

Who is the Leader of

Your Pack?

CHAPTER
–Three–

Have you ever stopped and thought about what it means to be a leader? Responsibilities of leadership are vital to the success of any group whether it be canine or human. What type of leader are you? This is very important to consider because it affects not only your attitude and confidence but the rest of the group as well. We can learn a good deal about leadership from our dogs and use this information to help to change our life for the better.

Leadership means responsibility. This means the responsibility of service to others – the ones who follow you. Great leaders inherently know this – they understand that the benefits of leadership also bring with it great requirements. So, what are those requirements in great leadership? Let's take a look at the next two examples and then we will answer those questions.

While I was dealing with Spanner and the tragedy of Phoenix, I began to see how my life needed to change. My back still hurt because of my firefighting career. I was also dealing with issues of depression and post- traumatic stress disorder (PTSD) as a result of that time. It became very difficult to open a door to a new life when the last door still hadn't fully closed. I did the best I could with moving on, but as anyone who has had PTSD can attest, it is not easy when that trigger hits and sends you to a place that is rough to handle. So some days went by and the fog of depression pulled me down. Some days would be hard to get out of bed, not just physically but also mentally from the results of the injury. Having the animals to care for helped greatly. I had to rise to the occasion for them because they had no one else to look after their needs. No matter how I felt, the animals always got tended to. In fact, the majority of my life's focus was on the animals. I hated to leave the property because I felt secure there with them. It was much safer that way, too. I did not need to deal with any of my past issues. I only had to be there for them. I was a very good functional depressive case. Looking back, I realize it was an extremely important time for me as well. It shaped who I am today, and it was a time to help me grow.

For many people in this situation, the death of Phoenix would have put them over the edge and caused them to leave the animals in someone else's care. Instead, it spurred me on. At the time it was anger, but I used it in a way to bring good out of it. This was the event that caused me to change directions with my refuge and open our doors to needy animals that crossed my path. I no longer worried about what other people said, and I had learned through the help of a great counselor that worry was a waste of time. So why bother letting whatever you are worrying about waste so much of your time? Years later, I learned even more how useless worrying really is and, in fact, how detrimental it really is.

Now, if an animal could touch my heart I knew it was brought to me for help. I did everything in my power to help it. That is about the time I saw a photo at the vet's office of three of the cutest little puppies that needed help. The woman was a client of the vet and had taken in a pregnant stray. The dog had seven pups, and the woman needed help finding homes for three of them.

At the time, I was not savvy about facilitating dog adoptions, but I knew we had the space and so I decided to help with one or two of the pups. I spoke to the woman and told her about the rescue organization. I explained that these pups would stay with us and have a great place to live. These seven were just adorable puppies. (Yeah, they all are, aren't they?) I knew we would take the brown one of the bunch and his name would be Fawkes after the phoenix in the *Harry Potter* books. We just could not decide which one to take as the second pup. The other choice was between a solid black pup and one with a star on his chest. Since we felt bad in choosing one and leaving the other alone, we took all three! The boy with the star was named Bennu after the Egyptian word for phoenix, and the third was called Tucson since it is a city near Phoenix. As you can see, we wanted to honor that little girl who helped me on my journey. Eventually, we took in all five pups as well as the momma dog. The woman who rescued the mother encountered an emergency situation and found herself in need of a place to stay as well. We were happy to be able to offer our help during this time. This was quite an undertaking for us since I had to leave town every other week for treatments on my back.

During this stressful time, one of the pups developed a little cold and the other pups got conflicting signals from my leaving and returning. Soon after the first pup became sick, the others fell ill as well. The puppies started fighting. These were some pretty serious fights, too. We could not get them apart. It was becoming a major concern and also a major point of stress and frustration. We wrote to Jan Fennell to ask her advice, and she pointed out the lack of leadership. This pack was in major upheaval with so much coming and going, illness and weakness from my injury. The pack lacked proper signals. During these fights, there was lots of shouting, and the anxiety it produced was almost as bad as the fight. I definitely lacked in leadership skills for my little wolf pack.

Sam, Frodo, Fawkes, Bennu, Tucson

Through a lot of hard work and learning first and foremost to be calm, we were able to get the "Brothers Five" back together. The woman who needed help, Quinci, eventually took the momma, Shelby, and the two boys, Sam and Frodo, to live with her. To this day, the five siblings can come together for a play date and romp and have a great time. In fact, Sam and Frodo are intact males, but it is not an issue. We have given them the proper leadership signs and we understand how to be calm, convincing, confident, and have the right attitude.

*"Leadership is practiced not so much in
words as in attitude and in actions."*
– Harold S. Geneen

PUPPIES, PUPPIES, EVERYWHERE

As life continued with the Brothers Five, their mom and Spanner, two more babies entered the scene...

One day while shopping at PETCO, I noticed some teenagers with tiny puppies. They were wandering around the store in a panic. Since I knew the store pretty well, I asked if they needed help. They told me that the mother had been hit by a car several days before and they needed to know how to feed the pups. They had already lost five babies and now three remained. I did not know what they were feeding the pups, but if they wanted those two to survive, then I knew they had to do something. I helped them to get all the supplies they needed, and we weighed the pups on the scale at the register. I taught them how to care for the pups and gave them my business card offering any additional help. Four weeks later, they called and asked if I could take the two puppies. We named them Navarre and Isabeau after the film, Ladyhawke.

The pups got sick at eight weeks old. A trip to the vet with the concern for Parvo went unheeded. After our experience with Phoenix, we followed a strict quarantine procedure, as well as a cleaning protocol. We thought we were safe, but little did we know just how easy it was to spread this terrible disease.

The vet sent us home with antibiotics and instructions to wait. Once again, we learned things the hard way. The situation worsened, and a second trip to the vet became inevitable. We demanded a Parvo test and the most aggressive treatment. Still, the vet sent us home with oral meds and told us to wait. I should have listened to my feelings from the start with the first vet trip. My instinct told me one thing, and my vibrations were in full swing to give me what I did not want. I focused hard on this illness and let worry creep in. We tried frantically to save these babies. Then it happened. Isabeau slipped into a coma, and we rushed to the Veterinary Emergency Clinic (VEC) that was 40 minutes away. About 15 minutes into the trip, our dear little Isabeau breathed her last breath. We pulled over into a service area and cried.

We still had sick little Navarre with us, so we turned around and drove straight to the regular vet and waited for him to open. Amazingly, the vet still wanted to give more oral meds and send us home with the dog, even after we stated that we wanted the best treatment. Leaving that vet office never to return, we took Navarre to the VEC in Orlando that evening. We slept outside in the car, so we could be close in case the unthinkable happened. I decided I was no longer going to be passive, instead, I was going to lead my pack. I needed to be strong for this little boy. He was still sick and also just lost his sister. It was only a month prior that he lost his mother and other siblings as well. Those changes in vibrations slowly turned things around for me. I told Navarre when we left him with the technician that I was right here and I would never leave him. He was safe, and I believed that he could pull through. Little Navarre went through a tough time but had great medical care and a fortuitous catch of a blood imbalance by one of the doctors at the emergency facility.

During the days, we took him to South Orlando Veterinary Hospital because the emergency vet was only open at night. Being permitted to stay with him in his little hospital cage, I stood by his side for eight hours to be with him. He looked like a little skeleton, but slowly he gained weight. After seven days and nights, this little boy came home. He was 9 weeks old and weighed only 4 pounds!

Navarre is now three-and-a-half years old and 45 pounds of love. The bond I have with Navarre is beyond words. I learned that I could not give him the human kind of love I wanted to. I needed to give him the canine kind of love he required. You see, when a dog is ill and you cuddle and act to comfort him, you are reinforcing the weak and stressed state the dog is in. You are also not acting as the calm, confident leader. Your comforting is not helping, but instead increasing weakness. You need to keep a reassuring hand on the dog without petting or stroking him; this will allow the dog to feel your strength in the situation.

Beginning to fully understand my journey in this life, I have a much better understanding now of how to choose a vet, doctor, surgeon, dentist, plumber, etc. I no longer let them push me in the direction that they think is the way to go. I research issues and go into a situation with a better understanding. I am more assertive and educated when it comes to finding help. I realized for the first time how important it is to be the leader of your pack. If puppies could go into outrageous fights over such chaos and lack of leadership, if levels of anxiety could skyrocket for a dog that has no leader, then there was something important to the situation. I also realized just how much the Law of Attraction relates to your leadership skills. The vibrations you give off will absolutely bring you greatness or disaster. Pay attention to your feelings. They are your unfailing guide.

After reading two of Jan Fennell's books, I became active in a well-respected dog training school that followed a kind and positive philosophy. Because I wanted to further my experience with dogs, I then took the first opportunity I had to travel to England. This was the beginning of the process of studying with Jan. I attended the foundation training course in England and then was invited back to attend the advanced course. I was now on my way to becoming a Dog Listener myself.

Throughout our journey together in this book, I will strive to help you be in harmony with your dog, as well as learn a few important life lessons. Harmony suggests that pack members want to cooperate and work together, just as wolves do while they hunt. This is a key factor to understand for a Dog Listener. Wouldn't you want this kind of relationship with your dog, one that is harmonious and tension-free? This next story is a cute little excerpt from a retired police dog handler and trainer who uses the "Amichien Bonding" method in the United Kingdom.

WHO IS IN CHARGE, OFFICER?

When my children were very much younger, my wife and I were going to the theatre and booked our usual babysitter, Sondra, another policeman's daughter. She was a very reliable babysitter and my three children all liked her. However, she was extraordinarily pretty and had a body... well – let's just say she had a body! Sondra was sought after by all the young men in town and quite a few of the older ones as well. She asked if she could bring her new boyfriend to keep her company on the night and we agreed.

Sondra and her boyfriend turned up at the appointed time and you could almost hear his hormones warming up, he couldn't wait to get rid of us. Off we went leaving three children and police dog Ben behind.

When we got home, we found all three children in bed asleep, a disgruntled-looking boyfriend, a smug-looking dog, and a laughing Sondra. She told us that every time the boyfriend started to get amorous, Ben would allow him to start putting an arm around her shoulders but anything other than that, Ben would stand up and put a front paw on each of the boyfriend's, thighs and stare him out.

Sondra told my wife she was happy, because she realized she was not as keen on this fellow as she had first thought. At the end of the evening, she told him that she would not be seeing him again. She went home with her babysitting money and he went off, presumably to have a cold shower. It really is important to establish leadership!

Robin Glover, Hampshire, England
www.robinglover.com

In Robin's case, his babysitter was glad the dog took the role of leader. However, you can easily see it isn't always such a great idea.

Establishing which type of leader you are is a big debate these days. Many "experts" find themselves with traumatized dogs that appear to calmly submit. What has happened is a state of learned helplessness has been created. The antiquated "alpha roll" is one technique still used today where a dog is rolled onto his back, exposing his belly, and held there by the throat. Early researchers stated that this roll was a means by which alpha wolves established dominance. Later, however, it was discovered that this was very misleading. It was an appeasing gesture on the part of the subordinate. It was done willingly by the subordinate and never by force. You can easily see this in many dog packs at a local dog park. In fact, a wolf would only be flipped on its back by force by an animal intent on killing it. This makes the violent struggles and the psychological trauma from dogs that have been flipped completely understood. This is not the behavior of a wolf establishing dominance but of one intent on serious harm. Look into the eyes of a dog as it is flipped and notice the fear. This is not a way of establishing a willing and cooperative pack with your dogs. Now, what you *will* see in wolves and dogs is a pinning behavior similar to what wrestlers do. A dog in play or in a fight holds its body weight down onto the other dog. It is a very different situation from the trainers' technique of the "alpha roll".

Dr. David Mech is one of the most respected wolf researchers in the world. What he has noted is that, in the wild, wolf packs are generally made up of a single monogamous breeding pair and their offspring. Large wolf packs may include more than one breeding pair. When the pups become old enough, they go off to form their own pack with their own territory. In other words, a wolf pack is not a rigid hierarchy but a family. The "alpha" parents make the decisions and keep the pack in harmony. Just as any family unit, when stressors are low, there is little conflict. If stressors are high, you may find hierarchical disputes that are mediated by the parents.

Many people think you must dominate an animal in order to tame it or to become its leader. This causes problems. Dogs are no more dominant animals than people are, and they react to domination the same way we do – just with slightly more fang and growl. Based on their personalities, they will either accept the lower position or make a stand of their own. There are also those that fall in the middle of the two extremes. The alpha roll we spoke of is one way to dominate, but there are many other ways trainers use to accomplish it. Dogs react to it the same way humans would: traumatized and learned helplessness that makes them broken, obedient, and complacent. This is no way to treat a dog, just as it is no way to treat a person.

"Until he extends the circle of his compassion to all living things, man will not himself find peace."
– Albert Schweitzer

Dr. Sophia Yin, a professor at the University of California School of Veterinary Medicine, as well as a member of the American Society of Veterinary Behavior, has said, "Yes, owners should be calm and assertive, and it is true to help dogs we need to be in charge. But dominance and leadership are two different things. Dominance is defined as the use of force to gain priority access of the things you want, so animals compete for food, toys, and favorite resting areas by fighting. Leadership is the ability to convince others to do things they normally would not do otherwise. A person can be a leader by bullying or by providing incentives and rewards; in other words convincing followers you're working for the same goals. Would you rather follow a leader like Castro or Gandhi? It is no different for dogs."

Writer John Stevens had this to say about two of his dogs on his blog, *Thoughts of Johnny V,* "Hekkla obeyed me out of fear for what might happen if he did wrong. Sarah obeyed me out of love. She wanted to do everything possible to please me. The result was a bond that was closer than the one with fear. It had nothing to do with the dog. Both were prepared to love me unconditionally. It had everything to do with the attitude that I brought to the relationship".

"Since this great revelation, I have tried to apply this principle to my life. It all fits in with the belief that love never fails and that there is no fear in love."

In the wild, you may see a bully-type leader, but they are not long lived. Take for example the story about the death of legendary Wolf 40 in Yellowstone National Park. Wolf 40 was part of the Druid Peak Pack. The night before her death, she was spotted displaying her usual dominance over the other wolves and their pups in the pack. There are several theories surrounding Wolf 40's death. Many speculate she was killed by the other females in the pack that she was once so harsh with. There were three other females, all with pups. No matter the cause, this story is a good example of how leadership can be challenged and another wolf can assume the role of leader within the pack. Acting harsh to show your dominance does not show any capability as a leader. As in the previous example, it will never truly be known why Wolf 40 was killed, but the subordinates may simply have had enough.

On the other side of the coin is Wolf 21. He was actually Wolf 40's mate for a time prior to her death. He was one of Yellowstone's greatest wolf leaders after the reintroduction of the wolf in 1995. He is a prime example of how successful a kind and nurturing leader can be even in the wilds of a wolf pack.

Wolf 21's Story

Born among the first litter of wolves in the Yellowstone area in almost 70 years, Wolf 21 was among the eight pups at the Rose Creek wolf pen in Lamar Valley in 1995. Having left the "fold" of his natal Rose Creek pack, he quickly became one of the most recognized wolves in Yellowstone as the alpha male of the Druid Peak Pack. He was featured on *National Geographic's* "Wolves – A Legend Returns to Yellowstone." Cinematographer Bob Landis actually filmed his acceptance into the pack as the new alpha male. This was the first time acceptance was ever observed in the wild and also a first to be caught on camera. As alpha male of the Druid Peak Pack, Wolf 21 helped establish what was to become one of the largest packs ever recorded, an unprecedented 37 wolves. A strong leader and gentle father, he was even seen on occasion allowing his pups to knock him down and pin him... something that you do not do to an alpha wolf.

Wolf 21 died at the Druid Pack's summer rendezvous site in June 2004 of unknown natural causes; he was 9 years old.

The next two stories demonstrate just how establishing leadership can be achieved in that kind way, the way Wolf 21 would handle his pack. Jacqui Murk's story is from Ireland, and Penny Locke's story is from California.

Unstuck and Relaxed

Michelle contacted me because she had some trouble with her two dogs – a Bernese Mountain dog named Bailey and a Newfoundland named Archi. Bailey was very nervous and hyper when the doorbell rang. Archi was very afraid and hid a lot. He was also nervous around people.

Michelle was a teacher, and when she went to work, her sisters took care of the dogs. Her sister also had a dog called Lotty, a Corgi. The sisters lived together in one big house with their husbands and several children. It was a very hectic household. The dogs looked a bit lost. Bailey was almost stuck to Michelle's leg, and when I asked her to move to another chair, Bailey followed her. I told her that Bailey looked very tired and was not relaxed. When somebody came to the door, Bailey started to growl, and I asked Michelle to remove him from "the pack" for a few moments. When she opened the door to let him out, he growled at Archi. Again I asked Michelle to remove him. The second time she opened the door, the dog growled again but not the third time. Archi seems very confused and did not know what his part was in this busy family household. The dogs would benefit a lot from the "Amichien Bonding" method because they would know their place within the pack. It was also very important that the dogs first relax before they are interacted with, and then it was always on Michelle's or her sister's terms. The ladies both understood that the dogs did not see a leader in the household and that they would have to fill that role. Lotty was a very old doggie, and most of the day she just slept.

Michelle told me it took three days before Bailey settled down. The following day (after the consultation), Bailey and Archi growled at each other and for another eight days. This has now stopped, and Bailey is "unstuck" from Michelle as well. He is also not growling at visitors anymore. The tired look has been lifted from Bailey. Archi is much more relaxed and does not show any more of his old behavior. She is now a very happy leader with dogs who are relaxed and happy to follow her.

Jacqui Murk, Ireland
Dog Listener

Our society mimics a wolf pack in many ways. Which of these men would you want to lead your pack, Adolph Hitler, Saddam Hussein, or M.K. Gandhi? All have mass followings, but for me I would not like to find myself in the Hitler or Saddam group. One group will most willingly want to follow you, while the other group is sure to go along for a quiet life. It is quite possible to be the peaceful leader and have an amazing dominion following you. In fact, this is exactly how to cause the laws of the universe to flow in the direction we all want. You will attract good things and move in a great rhythm. Remember Wolf 21's legacy of being the leader of the largest, most successful pack in Yellowstone history. The universal laws worked well for that kind leader. What were the final results for the two leaders mentioned above? Not as successful as Gandhi. The vibrations given off bring more things to continue fulfillment. The cause will bring an effect we can look exuberantly toward.

"If you can keep your head when all
about you are losing theirs..."
– Rudyard Kipling

This first line of Kipling's poem, *If*, personifies what dogs are looking for in their leaders. In reality, we are all looking for this in our leaders, including the wolf. These are the generals, presidents, CEOs, managers, parents, and anyone else that we want as leaders. I believe that by watching these majestic creatures we can definitely see first how to be the best pack leader for our dogs and apply this to our own lives and take the human condition to a higher level.

Penny's story takes place in a shelter facility and shows that no matter what situation a dog is in, the right leaders can make things much better for the dog in question.

EXPERIENCING THIS WORLD WEARING A DIFFERENT HAT

I have always had a soft spot for German Shepherds, so when a particularly striking black female shepherd came to our local shelter, I wanted to get to know her. She was called Black Beauty, and the name suited her well. About a year old, she was frantic, desperate for someone

to show her what was going on in a way she could understand. She was wild. She jumped up at everyone, whether you got close to her kennel or tried to get inside. She barked constantly and was in a serious state of anxiety.

I used the Amichien Bonding in all my interactions with the dogs in the shelter. Even Black Beauty's current state of mind, I knew I could get her to understand that she did not have to be so anxious, because I would be a leader for her. With the approval of the staff, I began to gesture eat with her, which meant I came in almost every day and fed her using Jan Fennell's protocol. When I approached her kennel, she barked and jumped wildly, with that "something could be in it for her" idea. I stepped away, aborting my efforts rather than fighting my way into her kennel, which would only reward her behavior. I made myself scarce; she was unable to see me. Once she quieted, I returned, only to have her repeat her antics. I retreated again to have her, I swear, put together that whenever she barked and jumped up, I went away with her bowl of food. Now, I just love to watch dogs figure out what they have to do in order for them to get what they want. My resolve was certainly tested, but I knew that if I gave into her behavior, then I would not have made very good leader material. Thus, no respect would have been won through the exercise. The same protocol allowed me to open the kennel door without her jumping up or pushing into my personal space. If she did at all, I left the kennel. I wanted to teach her to think, "If I jump up, she leaves, not good". Black Beauty was learning an all-important skill of self-control. It would have been easy to give up at this point. I saw it all the time; people with limited time or so desperate to get the dogs out they would excuse all the bad behavior in the kennels only to have them continue outside as well. I have plenty of resolve, and Black Beauty benefited from this.

I repeated the coming and going as much as needed. I knew that time invested here meant on my next visit that her antics would be shorter and shorter.

I continued gesture eating with her for the next week, with help from some fellow volunteers. I used the same protocol with her for walks, too. She had to wait until I was the first out of the kennel, through the door to the outside world. She gained self-confidence since she knew what was needed of her and she did not need to "lead".

While easily combining the status, feeding and walk elements of Amichien Bonding into my dealings with Black Beauty, I established a way to work with her on perceived danger, as well. This for her was the approach of any other dog toward her considerably large personal space.

In a side yard next to the main door leading from the kennel area to the outdoors, I set up a super-sized crate with a large blanket covering it. I waited with Black Beauty, who wore a collar and dragged a leash so I could come into her space safely. Setting this up, as the morning walks were beginning, gave me lots of opportunities to practice showing her there was no threat and that I would handle everything. As a dog was brought out by a volunteer for a walk, Black Beauty dashed over to the fence, barked loudly, and lunged at the other dog. Calmly, I walked over, took hold of her leash, guided her into the crate, shut and locked the door, and covered it with the blanket. She barked and scratched at the door. After a few minutes, with me just looking around and minding my own business, I let her out on her own recognizance, ignoring her completely for a couple of minutes before I called her over for a hug and stroke. I repeated the isolations as needed, and soon she learned how to remain with me, her surrogate pack. Through the isolations I was able to say to her, "I see no problems or threats in these dogs going by, and as leader I have decided that nothing needs to be done about them". It was exciting to see Black Beauty go from a full-on lunge, to looking at the dog, looking at me, and doing NOTHING. Yeah! I knew with the right and clear information she could make the right choice.

After a couple of weeks, she was much calmer. People could take her out for a walk, as long as they followed the protocol.

I also spent quality time with her. Our quiet time allowed me the opportunity to teach her about my personal space and status. Taking a folding chair into her kennel with my book, I sat, read, ignored her, pushed her away from my personal space, stroked and groomed her. The attention was always on my terms, not hers. If she nudged me, pushed against me, or licked my hands, I would ignore her and push her away, without saying a word. Only when she respected my personal space by stopping this behavior, did I invite her into my space and pet her.

After only a couple of weeks of working with her, with help from other volunteers, we saw great changes. I remember just shortly before she went to her forever home, I saw a couple take her out for a walk on the campus. The man had had several German Shepherds, so he knew "how to <u>make them do</u> what he wanted". He was yanking at the collar, shouting harshly at her. I was so shocked and upset I ran to the adoptions desk and asked if someone would walk with them so he would stop bullying her. So much for building trust in humans! I was so upset that my body physically shook. Fortunately for both Black Beauty and the couple, the man decided, "She did not have the temperament they were looking for".

Black Beauty was a dog that out of necessity had taken on the leadership role, as she thought she needed to for survival. With Amichien Bonding, she was able to see the world with a different hat on, that of being a relaxed and carefree dog.

Penny Locke, California
www.allabout-canines.com

An effective leader follows the three "C's" – Calmness, Consistency, and Confidence. Just by following the first one, calmness, our lives will become much better. Traffic accidents, road rage, shootings, murder, and divorce would decrease. Parenting, care of our elders, and many other aspects of the human race would greatly improve. Good health is also important to a leader. You can't lead your pack if you aren't well enough to make decisions and protect your followers. This is another reason why living in a tranquil manner is a must for leaders. Learning to live our lives in a calm manner helps keep our pulse and blood pressure rates lower, and our patience will increase to aid these things along the way.

Consistency is an area that will help us learn to develop the right mindset. Once we have changed our mindset we can transform our habits, and we change our old paradigms by a consistent effort over the course of time.

The third "C," confidence, is a must for all leaders. Confidence is required to make decisions. If we are unsure, we then cause negative vibrations to help bring the things we do not want in life. Confidence is not easy in a new situation, particularly in our first experience as a leader. If we paint a mental picture of the type of leader we want to be and then see ourselves as that leader, we can improve our confidence. Use other people's experience to gain your confidence. Study, read, and visualize yourself as the confident leader you truly are. Now take a moment and remember a certain behavior of your dog that caused you in the past to lose your cool and get frustrated. Now remove that negative image and replace it with one where you are a calm, consistent, confident leader for your dog. Once you have accomplished this with your dog, you are ready to implement this in your dealings with the people in your life. Think of the difference it will make in your relationships with your family, children, spouse, employees, or bosses.

Decision-making is an important role of a leader of a pack. If we give the wrong signals, our dog will take on the roll of decision-maker. This is how important decision-making is to the dogs. If they do not sense that we are capable of the role of leader, they will take on the role themselves. Since we have the knowledge of what it takes to be a good leader and we have the ability to change our paradigms (i.e., our "old" way of thinking), we can decide to give our dog what it needs and take that with us. We can make any decision with confidence because we are a leader.

Pat Roberts reminisces about the beginning of her and Monty's new relationship with a dog that helped them on another language expedition. Instead of "listening to horses", they learned how to "listen to dogs".

Cody Comes to California

Jan gave a good description of Cody to Monty and me. She visited us shortly after I picked Cody up at the Los Angeles airport on a flight from Chattanooga, Tennessee, where he had been bred. Jan observed Cody for a half-day or so and then asked us, "Do you know what you have here"? Monty and I looked at one another and both replied, "A puppy"! Jan said, "Yes, he's a puppy. But he is also an alpha male, a total clown, and way off the charts in intelligence". Monty and I looked at one another and then asked, "So"? Jan further explained to us that when dogs have an alpha personality combined with the brilliance of mind along with his other characteristics, you have a recipe for disaster, or a lot of hard work ahead until he gets past a dog's terrible two's.

Jan proceeded to tell us that the next couple of years in our lives were going to be filled with challenges that we probably never had experienced with our previous two Australian Cattle Dogs, Jay and Reno.

It seems they were quite normal when compared to Cody, although we wouldn't have thought them ordinary in any sense of the word during the time we shared our lives with them.

Both Monty and I love "blue dogs" or "Queensland Heelers", as they are so often called. They are a breed that has been specifically bred to work cattle and sometimes sheep. They are great companions, wonderful watchdogs, but not so great with small children. They exhibit a lot of their wild instincts in that they are fascinated by children and seem to want to stalk them. As Cody has mellowed with age, he seems to accept the fact that young ones move around a lot and sometimes in rather rapid motion. If children ignore him, he acts like he wants to make friends, and from then on he will enjoy their company.

Even choosing Cody was a bit of drama in our lives. I inquired and was told that a specific breeder was producing the best Australian Cattle Dogs available in the United States, and I contacted her because naturally I wanted the best. She immediately e-mailed me photos of the litter she had at the time. I fell in love with a puppy that had two black-ringed eyes, and was promptly told that the pup I chose was already sold. The only male available was not suitable for showing and breeding, which made him a good companion dog. Not only did he not have the two black-ringed eyes I wanted, he had no specific characteristics other than a white-tipped tail. Even though he was less than perfect, we wouldn't get much of a price break.

I e-mailed the breeder notifying her that I wanted to wait for the next litter to see what would be available at that time. She responded by telling me that this was the last litter for the year and I would have to wait for over a year to obtain a pup from her. She was a good salesperson though; she kept sending me more photos of this cute little pup with nothing special of note in physical characteristic except his gregarious *character, which appeared with frequency in the images. With each photo, she managed to capture a bit of his outgoing, expressive personality, and it wasn't long before I succumbed and committed to purchasing a very expensive dog that wasn't even the show dog I thought I wanted.*

He made the trip to California like a world-seasoned traveler and slept all the way in the car to Solvang during the two-and-a-half hour trip. A fat, little fluffy ball of grey fur with the one white tip on his tail, he was adorable and, naturally, I fell in love immediately. He seemed like a Cody, and that's what we named him. I decided to crate him after reading all the latest information on "how to raise a puppy" despite the fact that we had dogs before and had never used the crate. He took to his regimen and was fairly easy to housebreak considering his puppy-hood. However, from the very beginning, he showed strong tendencies to want things his way.

One of his first trips off the farm was to visit the local small animal veterinary hospital for his shots and first examination. Imagine sitting in the waiting room and hearing, "Cody Roberts to the examination room"? His first vet check showed him to be more than healthy. But since we were going to have him altered, I was told that I should watch his weight, for he was already a chubby little boy. As a consequence of that admonition, I returned home with "chubbins" and attempted to get him to climb up on a balance scale we have for our own use. That was a joke! He wasn't having anything to do with a contraption that moved and made strange noises.

When I tried to sit him down, keep him there and work the balance bar at the same time. Monty watched the procedure and commented, "Why don't you just teach him how to get up on it and weigh himself"? I looked at him skeptically. But I wasn't doing any good the way I was handling the situation, so I thought to myself, why not? I had already discovered that Cody loved cheese. And, if I didn't realize this before, what happened next reinforced how much he loved cheese! It took about 15 minutes to convince Cody to climb up on the scale, sit down, and wait for the reward. It was a "piece of cake", or should I say, piece of cheese? He would do anything for me if I rewarded him with a "good boy" and a bit of cheese.

This was the first of the many accomplishments Cody achieved over the next couple of years. Monty and I have had great fun teaching this brilliant Mr. Personality all sorts of interesting procedures. The first trick after the scale was to learn to sneeze on cue. I didn't teach him. He just sneezed one day and I praised him and reinforced it by running to the refrigerator for a piece of cheese. That was it. From then on, if he thought it might bring him a bite of cheese, he'd walk up to you, sit down on his haunches, look you in the eye, and give out with a huge sneeze.

Cody gives high fives with his right paw, sits up on his hind legs, balances a piece of cheese on his nose while sitting until the word "okay" is given, then tosses it in the air, and catches it. He can open the latched door of his crate as well as close it. He plays dead when you say "bang" to him. He can crawl on his belly to sneak up on a piece of cheese without touching it until the word "okay" is said, and he can even stand on his hind legs and do the cha-cha.

One of his stranger traits is to take his sheepskin bed out of his crate and carry it around the house with him, like a child with a security blanket. When he gets to the spot somewhere in the house, usually the room I am working in, he takes his front legs and paws and goes through a motion that appears he is wrapping his blanket up into a small ball. This is when he will lay down with it in his mouth for long periods of time.

He might not be a "Skidboot", the blue dog star of the Internet, but he certainly comes close. In fact, there are times when we find ourselves spelling out words in an effort to keep him from knowing what we are saying. I better not come out of the bedroom with my purse because that will elevate his adrenaline. He knows this means I'm going somewhere and he wants to go. If I come out of the bedroom rolling a suitcase, it's depression time. He hates it when I leave; however, he tolerates Monty leaving because he knows I'll be there. When I take Cody to the office, he will patiently wait for me until he feels that it's time to go. Enough of this boredom! He will come to my desk, sit up in a begging fashion, and look me in the eye as if to say, "Please, can't we leave now?". He is working hard all the time to make the decisions and be the leader, just as Jan said he would.

We sometimes wonder, "What on earth were we thinking"? After not having a dog for over five years, I think we forgot that they are a big responsibility, with housebreaking, teaching them boundaries in the house, not to chase horses and/or deer, and all the other things that must be addressed with raising a young pup. How quickly we forgot that bringing a dog into our life is rather like having another child. One must now come up with babysitters for the dog, as well as the house. Monty is seldom home, therefore he hasn't really changed his lifestyle much with the arrival of Cody in the late spring of 2004; but I feel my life has definitely been altered. In the end, it is all worth it for what I have learned.

Cody has brought new energy and life to our once-tranquil existence. Cody's really livened things up on Flag Is Up Ranch. He's a dynamo, as anyone who meets him will quickly point out and those of us who live with him certainly agree. But he's a lovable companion who loves to entertain our many guests with his latest tricks, his outgoing personality, and all the dynamics that go along with his strength of character. And above all, he really is a natural-born ham. He has shown me that it is necessary to establish leadership with a brilliant animal. He takes his responsibilities so seriously that I believe had we not shown him through our actions that he can relax and not worry about us constantly he would be a very disturbed dog. What we have learned through Jan's patient explanations is that a super-intelligent dog that wants to protect his family will fret if he deems his way isn't being followed. A dog's way of fretting can manifest itself in many forms; but, believe me, most of their actions in trying to keep "their world" safe can be counterproductive to living with them in a relaxed fashion.

At first, we thought it rather drastic to insist that we always go through a door first, to control a dog's eating by our actions (explained in detail in The Dog Listener, *Jan Fennell's first book), and to use the other means of establishing our leadership and allowing Cody to be a companion without the fear of failure. It was explained to us that if we don't convey this to our dogs then they are in a constant state of stress. It's been amazing to see the changes in Cody since we began to practice these techniques with him. He's more responsive to our wishes because we have established ourselves as leaders and he can just be a dog.*

Has he changed our lives? Yes, and the changes are definitely worth all the effort it takes to keep him happy and healthy. It took some time and work, but giving him what he needs in order to see us as the leaders of his pack has allowed Cody to shine. He's a fun-loving, affectionate dog that has strong likes and dislikes. He's definitely a family dog when it comes to true affection. He never forgets someone, and this can be both good and bad. It's bad for the pool maintenance man who comes once a week and somehow got on Cody's bad side. But it's great for the family and close friends, some of whom he might not see for a month or so. He gives me unconditional love, and that's my Cody, who started out to be what Monty wrote a poem about, the "Wrong Dawg", but he's ended up to be the best doggone dog you could ever hope to live with.

Pat Roberts, California
www.patrobertssculptures.com

If we want to be the best leader for our dogs, we must have the right mindset. No matter where we are in the moment, we have to be the best leader possible. This is paramount for us to be successful. Now, thinking positive thoughts is not enough. We need to truly believe that we are the best leader. By doing this we are creating a vibration that will bring us what we want. When we combine the correct attitude with true belief, we will see results.

As the leader, we are responsible for the safety and well-being of our pack. Our attitude must reflect a responsibility for our actions. It is not our dog's fault that he tore up a sofa cushion, nor was it her fault that she growled at the postal carrier. It was our fault. We should take responsibility for our dog's actions. At some point in the past the right signals were not given to the dog. Changing our paradigms will enable us to make a decision to do what it takes to be the right leader for our dogs. Then we will be responsible for our dogs relaxing on the cushions and for licking the postal carrier.

Our attitudes consist of our thoughts, feelings, and actions. So, if you think you are the leader for your dog and you truly believe it, then you take the correct actions to become the leader and you will be successful. If any one of these ingredients is missing, you will not succeed. Thoughts are great, but if you do not believe them then your actions will not matter. The same is true with action; all the correct thoughts will mean nothing. They will only be deeds without substance if you do not believe your thoughts. Repeating this process changes your paradigms, and the moment you apply this to your life, *wham-o*, you have success. Remaining calm, consistent, and confident allows a change for the better. You are actually leading yourself to a higher place.

CHAPTER
–Four–

Crikey! Danger,
Danger, Danger

CHAPTER
–*Four*–

Animals are in our lives to help us, so it is only right that we should be concerned for their feelings. Emotions bind different beings together. If dogs felt no emotion, then we would not have the connections that we do. We give, they give back. Dogs are good caretakers and work very hard at looking after their human babies when they take on the role of leader. The emotional toll it can take on a dog can be amazing. Maxi is a example of a dog that lost its children and had to deal with a great emotional burden.

I met Maxi after her owner called me looking for a place to put her for a year while he and his family rebounded from a financial hardship. I offered to foster this 7-year-old Great Dane mix, and they promised to help with a small monthly contribution. This family drove away in tears, and the problem was just beginning for Maxi. As they drove off, I realized how devoted this dog was to her babies who were leaving her. She was given all the wrong signals and felt it was her job to care for the family. Maxi paced all night. She did not sleep, and when she finally settled she would get up at the slightest noise. The constant lookout at the door was a sad sight. From her point of view, not only was she in a strange place but the kids were gone too.

The despair in her eyes was apparent, and soon afterward depression sunk in. Maxi stopped pacing only to lay on the floor by the window. After three days, I thought she would eat. She finally took a few nuggets after four days. The lack of food and anxiety took its toll. Maxi dropped some weight, which actually put her in a much more acceptable range because she was overweight when she came to us. It was hard to watch her constant panting and the wide-eyed look on her face. All I could do was keep the pressure off and show her she did not need to be concerned about me or have to look after me. The way to help a dog with this is by refusing eye contact and giving them space. I remained nearby performing activities that had no connection to her. I did not speak much, and if she refused to come to me I did not force it, nor did I go to her. I was simply a calm presence, there to show her I had no concern. My attitude and feelings were relaxed and positive. I did not feel sorry for her because that was not going to help her now, anyway. I simply took care of her needs and was there for company.

Maxi loosened up after a few weeks, but it took a long time for her to stop looking for her family. Maxi is a testament to the level of loyalty of the canine species. The people never stayed in contact with me, and I was never able to contact them. It took a long time, but Maxi did eventually find a great new home that would keep her for the rest of her life. Even though I know that dogs live in the moment, the human side of me still wonders if she "misses" her kids and if they show up in her doggie dreams.

Unfortunately, many people do not realize the depth of despair a dog can suffer simply by giving them the wrong signals. If I had continued to into Maxi signals that I, too, needed to be cared for, it may have pushed her over the edge. She may have shut down or developed a severe case of separation anxiety. Maxi was proof of how seriously dogs take their role of caretaker when given to them. If we look to Maxi, she is a testament to motherly instinct. I learned just how important it was to keep my own nurturing feelings aside. In the situations when I was a child with our new puppy Moses, or when Navarre was sick and in the hospital, I gave in to my human nature to nurture. Now remember, nurturing is fine, but the key is at the appropriate time.

Let's take a few minutes at this point to review the four key areas where we can show our dogs our ability to lead them. This is an abbreviation of Jan's method, but it will give you an understanding.

Reuniting After a Separation

The alphas in the wolf pack return after a separation and move through the group without acknowledging any members until the leaders are ready. When you have been separated from your dog for a few hours or even a few minutes and the dog rushes to greet you, it is easy to fuss over them. In fact, most people do, and by doing this we are inadvertently telling our dog that we are not the leader. Then he is free to invade our body space whenever he feels like it. Instead, when you walk in, *ignore your dog* until he leaves you alone! No matter what he does, if he jumps up, barks, whines, or runs around and bring you toys, *do not say a word or make eye contact,* just act as if you have not noticed. Using this "reuniting protocol" will keep the pressure off the dog.

Now jumping on you can be hard to ignore, especially with a large dog. In this case, gently push him off but without eye contact or speaking. Depending on your dog, the first time you do this could take a few minutes or even a couple of hours before he gives up and leaves you alone. Don't give up! The rewards will be worth it.

PERCEIVED DANGER

When your dog goes wild at the postman or any other visitor, he is warning you of possible danger. This is the role of a good pack member – to alert the leader. It is up to the leaders to decide how to deal with the situation. Acknowledge his assistance in protecting the pack by thanking him in a friendly, happy, confident tone of voice. If this does not quiet him down, go to him, thank him again, and look at what he is alarmed by. Bring him away from the door or window. If at this point your dog continues to bark, then the third strike means you are out! Now, you would separate your dog from the pack by putting him into another room, showing him the consequences of his actions! Leave him there until he has calmed down and stopped barking. When he rejoins the pack, he is once again ignored until he settles down.

Separating your dog from the pack is a strong message to the dog. As a pack animal, there is safety in numbers. They want to stay together. To show the dog in a natural way, without force or harshness that you are the decision-maker, isolating him for a few minutes is the key. You may need repeated sessions until he makes the full association of what behavior is causing the separation.

THE HUNT/THE WALK

In the wild, the alphas decide when to go on the hunt, and they start the charge off in the lead. It is important that you, too, go through the door to the big wide world first. You may need to do some preliminary work indoors before your dog is ready for the big wide world. Heel work and recall should first be taught off lead (and you can use a food reward). Work in your home, then the garden, before venturing outside the front door. Once the basics have been taught and the dog is happy to do these for you, you are ready to go out. If the dog starts to pull, *stop* and wait until the dog calms down. You may only be able to move one step at a time, but the instant the dog pulls remember to *stop.* You may even back up a few steps to bring the dog back to your side. The key is not shouting commands, but remaining calm. If the dog is unruly, return to the house, remove the lead, and leave it for about 10 minutes before starting again. This must be repeated, even if you do not leave the front lawn for a walk until the dog learns that if he pulls he does not go out. Always be calm, do not yank on the lead. As you progress on the walk, if the dog gets ahead of you, then calmly change direction and continue that pattern until the dog walks with you. Remember as you go: stop, start, and change direction.

One important note about the walk – if you are not seen as the decision-maker by your dog, you should be doing only the preliminary work at home and in the garden. Venturing out with your dog is *not* a necessity. It is only pertinent when both you and your dog can be happy, and you are in control. Remember, in the wild the wolves do not actually go out on a walk; they are going on a hunt. The animal that does not know when it will eat next is not going to needlessly waste energy. To keep our dogs lives enriched, stimulate their minds with games and fun play. If you are happy and in control and the dog enjoys the walk, then by all means have at it, but pay attention to the temperatures as well as the pads of his feet for his safety. Also pay attention to the length of the walk. Your first walk should never be for two hours. Everything should be a gradual buildup of time.

FOOD

After a successful hunt, the alphas would eat first to ensure their strength and continued ability to lead the pack. As pack leader, you eat first. When feeding your dog, it is a good reinforcement of your leadership if the dog sees you eating a cracker or cookie or piece of fruit first. It is not necessary for you to eat your entire meal first, and in fact that gap in time is too long to convey a strong message to your dog. After your tidbit, put the dog's bowl down and walk away, giving him space. If he refuses or leaves food in the bowl and walks away, pick up the food. Dinner is over. You retain control of the food, and he will eat again at the next meal.

The four areas I have highlighted here are just a very basic part of the Amichien Bonding method. There is much more to each area that I have not expanded upon. For the full version, please read *The Dog Listener* by Jan Fennell. I have only given the high points to give you the knowledge of what we are talking about in many of the stories. Now let's move on to looking at things a little more from the dog's perspective.

The late Steve Irwin had a coined phrase, "Crikey! Danger, danger, danger". He was a leader and a man who knew how to deal with those dangers. In the life of a dog, there are 1,001 dangers to be faced every day. A dog's primary concern is survival. If you truly look at the world through their eyes, you understand they are in a world they do not know. Let's look at things from a different point of view, one similar to what our dogs see in our world.

Through the Looking Glass

Imagine one morning you suddenly woke up and found yourself in a place where some larger species was speaking some strange language. You would not know what to fear and who to call friend. You would be very confused. In this alien world, you would be very concerned with *your* survival. As far as you know, the next thing around the corner could kill you. Now imagine if some "being" from this place coaxes you into a feeling of security. You are not exactly sure why, you are just sensing they mean you no harm. Since you cannot communicate with them, you must have some blind trust that they are taking you to a place where you will be safe. Your eyes are wide and your senses alert in case you judged wrong. Your heart rate speeds. After some time, they give you something to eat. Although it does not resemble anything you have seen before, it smells fine so you eat it. They give you an area to rest in, and since you are so tired from all this heightened sense of awareness, you find yourself drifting off.

The next day comes, and they guide you out into an area you have never seen. Things are flying past you at a very high speed and other beings are moving at a very quick pace. This is a very intimidating situation. Noises you do not understand are everywhere. Some of these other beings stop when they see you and rush up to you and pat you on the head. Out of surprise you allow it because you are really confused by all this. Then, all of a sudden, you see another human across the way. Your eyes light up and you quickly move in their direction. All the time your being is making some really loud sounds and chasing after you. When you get to the other human, its being jerks it away from you and turns to move off in the other direction. Your being catches up to you, grabs you by the back of the hair, and smacks your face! Now you are really scared. What is going on? You must now watch every step because your survival could be at stake.

As you walk back, you see another human running toward you! All of a sudden, a large object comes out of nowhere and almost hits her. You see this and your being is frantic. Another being comes running and seems frantic as well. As your being guides you away, it smacks you again on the head. All you can think is, "What was that for"?

This is a good example of not understanding a world around you. Now imagine living this story, if the "being" was able to communicate with you in a language you understood, things would be better. If you were alone without the being, navigating would have been very difficult. There was danger all around you. Who was friend and who was foe? It would have or could have been your life if you made the wrong move. All you have to go on is your instinct of the world and hope you get it right. But your world's rules may be very different, and those misunderstandings could cause you to get it wrong.

Often people may think that we humans occupy a plane far above the dog. It is just their perspective. However, when life begins to deteriorate, we return to basic instincts similar to our dogs. When people lose their comforts they resort to a natural instinct of survival. A few years ago, when Hurricane Katrina wreaked havoc on the city of New Orleans, the residents were forced to fall back on their survival mechanism. Looting, scavenging for food, and violence were a common sight on the news. This mass of people was desperately trying to fulfill their basic needs. In times of severe strife, all sense of law and order are abandoned. We are truly not so far removed from instinctual behavior. We should be willing to see things from our dog's point of view.

Making decisions is important to the dog's understanding as part of the survival instinct. They do it naturally, whereas we often struggle. We are equipped with an intellect that should allow us to make decisions easily, but often it gets in the way of our instinct. Firmly grounded in nature, the dog is given great tools for making decisions easily. We can benefit from their decision-making skills and can learn a thing or two from them about making decisions fast. Trust your instincts!

Nature has given dogs great senses of smell and hearing, primarily because they will be more adept at survival if they hear something or smell it before it knows they are there. This is a reason dogs are so great for drug enforcement or acting as police dogs. Dogs are presented with danger even before we know it is there. Let them be your guides while communicating to them that if they follow your lead you will make the right decision to protect them. As a result, you will have a very relaxed dog that lets you know when the mail has arrived!

Decision-making takes you far in your dog's life. It helps you prove your worth to him time and time again. For both humans and dogs, flight is the first choice decision in the sign of danger. This is often how a police chase begins. As a suspect sees the officer, they grow fearful and take flight. Never worry about leaving a situation you are not comfortable with, of course I don't mean with the police.

It is your decision to make as the leader for your dog, so flight is a viable option. The second option is to freeze. Simply pretend you do not see it. Then hopefully the danger will pass. You can see this in many dogs that shut down by fear and refuse to move. It is also evident when someone becomes overwhelmed at a task and they do absolutely nothing. The third option for dogs is to fight. This is the dog that is backed into a corner. You have taken away both its other options, and it is only left with fight to protect itself. Some dogs become so conditioned to the third response that they no longer use the first two. This is easy to see in humans as well. If you continually push someone, eventually they snap and "go postal". Some people are quick to go right to the argument or the fists, and this personality trait is also seen in dogs.

Every being, human or dog, has these initial instinctual responses, but the key is to learn how to control them. You should have confidence in yourself and your ability as a leader to make a sound decision fast. By fast I do not necessarily mean quick. This subtle difference is very important. Some decisions require you to make an informed decision, and to do that you may need to gather the facts. This may take time. What you want to avoid is making a decision so quickly that you are not making one that truly fits with your goals and desires. Also, slow decisions might be seen as indecision. When a dog sees you as leader, you should take the role very seriously because it means they trust you with their life. This is an honor given to us by another species and is something we should not take lightly. You need to remember, however, that just because a dog has chosen you leader today you will still have to prove your capability tomorrow and the next day and the next day and each day that follows. Remember that in the wild, in your dog's instinctual world, you never know when something may change.

The following story of Cheyenne is an example of a dog that continually asks questions about leadership. In her experience, she has seen just how important that is to her survival.

TROUBLE LOOMS

When I need supplies from the feed store, I have to drive through one particular town. On one of my recent trips, I had a feeling, which meant I was projecting the vibrations out there, that I was going to find a dog on this particular trip. As I drove it started to rain, and out of nowhere a little puppy ran into the lane. I quickly swerved to miss her and turned the car around to go back. Cars on the other side were stopping. The rain intensified, and you could see the indecision in her eyes. She submissive-peed and quickly ran down the road. She wanted to leave the situation, but as the rain came down harder, she turned and ran right to me. I picked her up and put her in the car. As I grabbed a towel for her, I saw that she was covered in fleas. *Immediately* this dog touched my heart. I knew she had come from a bad situation and she was not going back. She had large bite wounds on her back that seemed to be from another dog. Dog fighting is prevalent in the area in which I found her, and I often wonder if she was a bait dog.

I brought her home, treated her wounds, and set up a vet appointment at Powers Drive Vet Hospital in Orlando. The doctors, technicians, and staff there have all been invaluable to our rescue organization. Cheyenne came home to start a new life. After her quarantine period, I began to integrate her into the pack. She quickly made it apparent that she was very nervous around strange dogs. She barked alarmingly and it took some time for her to accept them. With a very careful and slow introduction, she acclimated to her new surroundings. Cheyenne quickly became a favorite but showed quite a few leadership challenges. She needed to be convinced that I could protect her, otherwise she was not interested in me at all. One thing that I also realized was just how important that position was to her. You could literally see her questioning my decisions. "Are you sure? I do not think so. It does not look right to me. You really think he is friendly?"

If she truly had been a bait dog, then her survival mechanism was in full swing and on high alert. She needed to trust completely, as if her life depended on it, as it did from her point of view. Wherever Cheyenne went, if she saw a strange dog, then she would immediately alert me to the danger. She needed extreme confidence to be assured she would be kept safe. For her to give me that type of confidence was truly an honor. There were still times when she attempted to make the decision on her own and then, in my kind way, I reinforced that I could make the right decisions for her and that all was safe. She kept me on my toes as a leader, and some days I do better than others in her eyes.

What I can say is now the value of the word "trust" has taken on a whole new meaning for me. If I trust you, believe me, it is a compliment. If you tell me you trust me, know that I will be there in any situation because I know how important trust is, thanks to Cheyenne.

RELATIONSHIPS WITHOUT TRUST?

Relationships without trust are relationships that create more emotional turmoil than satisfaction. Relationships are part of the human experience. We have them with our dogs, our families, our spouses, our coworkers, etc. They are always more rewarding when you have trust.

I assist the Shy Wolf Sanctuary in Naples, Florida, with wolf-dog evaluations that aim to rehabilitate certain dogs. The sanctuary does its best to help save an animal that is *very* misunderstood. Wolf-dogs are a product of people and the science of eugenics we spoke about earlier. Many calls come in to rescue shelters to take in a dog that is going to be killed by animal control because of its breed. They cannot help the fact that they have been bred, but they nonetheless suffer the consequences of people getting into something they are not prepared for. Wolf-dogs are persecuted about as much as pit bulls in this country. This animal is not wholly a wolf and it is not wholly a dog. It takes very specialized knowledge to give it the right guidance, care, and understanding.

When Deanna, a member of the Shy Wolf Staff, contacted me to do an evaluation on eight wolf-dog puppies and three adolescents, little did I know I would end up with three new rescues at my sanctuary. Simba, Nala, and Lady were just short of a year old. They were very shy and timid dogs, which is typical of wolves. The 8-week-old pups were adorable, and we were able to find homes for them without any problems. After several unsuccessful months trying to find a home for the adolescents, the family made a decision. The dogs needed to go. I managed to get some partial funding to put together a temporary containment for them. These dogs had been raised outside and may not ever transition to indoor dogs. We wanted to keep them together, which made it even more difficult to place them. They lived their entire one year of life together with their parents. We know the importance of the pack and felt it was in their best interest to keep them together.

Simba   **Nala**   **Lady**

They arrived at my facility and were extremely stressed. These were not the type of dogs that would easily bond with humans. Their trust had to be earned. I followed the method I knew worked best, using the reunite protocol. I sat in their enclosure and looked out at the property and they gradually came in closer for some quick sniffs. Any fast motion and they were off to the other end of the den. These dogs had not been abused or mistreated; they were simply different then a domestic dog. I made progress in a little under a month. I opened their enclosure and walked toward a large pasture. The more I did this, the more I noticed they acted like they did not care what I did. But as soon as I strayed a little too far from them, they came running. They followed me into the pasture and would romp and play with each other. It is a beautiful thing to watch when an animal shows complete bliss rolling in the grass and having a great time. I walked from one end of the pasture to the other as they played, and they followed me. When we were through, I walked back to their enclosure, and they followed me back inside. I took a lot of precautions before I actually let them loose. The whole time I was out with them, I never spoke a word. I did not need to, because I was still speaking their language.

The true test of their trust came almost eight months later. I transferred them into a much larger containment. Unfortunately, within an hour, they were able to bend the chain link. Wolf-dogs are notorious as escape artists, and they will test every inch of an enclosure. They are very smart and will also find the weakest points. Soon after, my neighbor called to tell me that he had three dogs in his yard and was wondering if they were mine. I peeked out the window and saw all three looking happy and thrilled. I grabbed some leashes and made my way to my neighbor's. I quickly called Lady, and she ran right for me. The other two headed up the driveway. This was unusual since Lady held a high rank with the pack and they almost always followed her. I clipped the leash on Lady and began a slow, comfortable walk up the driveway. It is a quarter mile to the road and they were making quick progress, but I could do nothing else. I knew you should never chase a dog you are trying to catch, because it usually causes him to continue to run away. About halfway up the driveway, using a sweet and pleasant tone, I said out loud, "Lady, come on, let's go".

As I turned to walk back home with Lady, Nala and Simba ran full steam past us and turned back to join us. There was lots of lip licking and wagging tails. I clipped the leashes on the other two escapees, and we slowed to a nice walk home. If those dogs did not fully trust me, they may very well have continued their frolic out to the road, a bad combination. If I had not stayed calm and confident that the situation would work out just fine, it could have also ended another way. Everything I learned from Jan benefited me and helped me to become the leader of the pack and gain their complete trust.

As wolf-dogs go, Simba, Lady, and Nala are pretty easy kids. My next adventure for Shy Wolf brought me a great pair that tested all my skills and really kept me on my toes.

OP AND NIKITA'S STORY

What a beautiful pair. OP stood for Obnoxious Puppy, and it fit him to a tee. Nikita was pulled from an SPCA shelter after spending eight months there. As a result of the long stay in such turbulent surroundings, she had major trust issues with humans. I knew they used a catch pole to get her out of her kennel and back in again. This girl was not going to be easy.

OP came as a stray a couple of days before we rescued Nikita. Miss Nikita attracted exactly what she needed, strength. The two were perfect for each other. He was a one-blue-eyed husky mix and she was a shepherd-wolf mix. Nikita had been through a lot, but now she could start her journey back.

Again I followed the reunite protocol with Nikita and kept the pressure off. I loved her from the very start. After all she had been through, it was amazing that she never once growled or bit anyone. "The big bad wolf!" Yeah, right.

I fought my instinct to not speak soft loving things to Nikita. I only did so when the time was appropriate. After several weeks of caring for her and showing her she was not threatened, we sat together and I was able to groom her. OP was a different story. He was a play machine. What a great body pillow he made. If I sat back quietly, OP would guide Nikita out of her shell and she would play with him. They loved to romp together. And she did tell him off a time or two as well. It took a lot of listening to Nikita to find out how much she trusted me. Anytime I tried to catch her, she tested me. Patience was a requirement for any dealings with her, and I had to stay completely relaxed. It took awhile, but when she would let me get close enough I could clip a lead on her. After I had worked with her for many months, Nikita began to trust me in a few small ways. I saw that as major progress considering how severely my species had let her down.

It was an amazing find, but the right people saw Nikita and OP's photos and knew these dogs should be with them. Nikita loves to join her new owner on the recliner to have a good cuddle and act like a lap dog. She now stands tall with the self-confidence she should have and the trust placed back in her human companions. Her tail wags for joy now. Both OP and Nikita found some awesome people to continue their care, and now they have a forever home with people they can trust.

Trust is key to any fulfilling relationship. When you have the right communication, trusting your pack members will be that much easier.

CHAPTER
– Five –

And My Dogs Says...
"So, What's in it for Me?"

CHAPTER
– *Five* –

Let's continue the discussion on decision-making. It is very important and it leads into the next few topics. How do you approach decisions? I used to make decisions by looking at the current circumstances and resources, allowing them to dictate whether I did something. The bank balance, my education, the calendar, my experience… the circumstances drove the decision. What I really wanted and why I wanted it was not in the picture.

What was I doing wrong? I had weak decision-making muscles. As I developed my Dog Listener skills, I started to understand what it meant to be the leader of my pack. I watched the dogs when a situation presented itself to them. I started thinking, how do dogs make decisions if left to themselves? Fast or slow? Remember we spoke in the last chapter about making fast decisions, but not quick ones. I began to pay close attention to interactions between the rescue dogs during play and meal times. It became obvious that the confident dogs all made decisions very fast. The dogs that had attitudes, some good and some bad, also made decisions fast. It was the insecure rescue dogs that were unable to make fast decisions. They appeared to be indecisive and really fought with their own issues of trust – in me and in themselves. Now, this was not a true experiment in the scientific sense of the word, it was just my casual observation. The dogs let their instincts guide them *almost* immediately in most situations. It taught me that we should do the same. In our world, some situations require a lot of information before a decision can be made. We should learn to cultivate the habit of relying on our instincts to make a decision *fast* as soon as we have the information needed.

Napoleon Hill interviewed 500 successful people in all fields and found that they had a common trait: successful people make decisions fast, and they seldom change them. They develop a clear image of what they want and then take action toward that goal or image.

The word "decision" comes from the Latin "de" (from) and "caedere" (to cut). We must commit ourselves to a result and then cut ourselves off from other outcomes. Let me explain. Are we afraid we might fail? We all make mistakes and fail. That does not make us a failure. Quitting makes us failures. A failure is simply not the right way. Failure is how we learn and gather what we need to achieve goals. Our mind and the universe require order before action. Decision brings order to the mind and allows it to focus on the actions that move us toward our goal.

This is not the first time we have spoken of the importance of decision-making. We have already seen in the last chapter how large a role it plays in selecting and following the pack leader. It is easy to speak of making decisions fast, but in practice it can be a bit trickier. One way to help is to prepare your decisions. If you know your goals, you can think ahead of some of the decisions you may need to make. Work on mentally rehearsing those decisions, and soon it will become easier. This is called making advanced decisions. Make advanced decisions by knowing what you want to do in a situation. Then when the situation appears, you will already have the decision.

Once again, we need to visualize our decisions and the outcomes. It is true that your brain works in pictures and does not know the difference between reality and fantasy. If you continually put pictures in your mind, you will find those pictures coming to pass. As we mentioned before, visualization takes practice. Spend some quiet time with your eyes closed and think about an empty movie theatre. Think about a movie that you want to create. It could be the movie of how fast and efficiently you make the decision when danger approaches your dogs. You see yourself walking your dog and dealing with that situation by walking in a different direction away from a possible threat. Maybe you have a dog that is "dog aggressive" on the leash. You can see your dog look up to you in a very relaxed way, you see yourself as the leader, calm and convincing and confident. You see things working the way you want them to work. Hear the sounds going on around you and *feel* the situation as if it were real. Practicing this process is an important step to a great life with your dog, as well as a great life in your world. It takes the frustration out of a situation that you already understand. It gives you the confidence to make decisions fast, based on your instincts and feelings. Not every situation can have an advanced decision, but with visualization, practice with fast decision-making and time, you will get the hang of it.

This next story is about a decision that many of us have had to make.

Tough Love

On Sunday, January 7th, the decision was made to put her down. There was an accident, and she had fallen 15 or 20 feet off the top of the training structure. She landed on her back. It was not a good place to fracture a vertebra. There was a 0% chance of the dog walking again. Even under extraordinary means, her quality of life would be minimal. It really was the only decision that could have been made. However, the pain involved in making that decision was pretty great.

In the search-and-rescue field, dogs are often asked to perform dangerous tasks. Most of the time it is fun, a great time bonding between canine and human partners.

Well, this was not one of the fun days. His canine partner was gone. She had been to seven federal deployments in her career, as well as a large number of deployments as a volunteer. She did everything that was asked of her, and more. She taught him about how to handle a dog. He showed her the search and rescue game. She helped train the task force and help show rescue crews from other parts of the world what a search-and-rescue dog could do.

In New York, she received an award for gallantry, the highest award in the world for animals. When it was time, she kissed his hand, closed her eyes, and went to sleep. She had also made her decision. She did not fight it. She was on to her next adventure.

This was the story of a search-and-rescue dog named Kinsey. Her handler, Bob Deeds, said "Love your dog, love what you do, and remember it can go away in a heartbeat".

Simply imagining yourself in that situation is very difficult. Many of us have been in similar situations where a tough decision had to be made. It is never easy, but the best interest of the animal is what is important.

Mia has been the impetus for one man to understand how to make a tough decision and the benefits it gave him. I met Mia and her foster dad, Harvey, about two years ago.

Mia had a rough start to life. Bounced around from one home to another, she suffered medical problems, and getting the poor dog to eat was a nightmare. She ended up in a foster home, which caused a lot of stress and worry. There were trips to the vet, and the foster owner spent a great deal of money to find something the dog could eat.

After some time and troubleshooting, he took a great step and made a fantastic decision. He put away all his worry about Mia not eating. You see, he was consumed by the fact that this dog would not eat. He would speak to me on the phone about it and ask for suggestions. He tried everything but could not make any breakthroughs. Deciding not to worry any longer about the situation helped, because he was no longer wasting energy, and it alleviated the pressure on the dog that surely she could feel. The foster dad decided to visualize Mia eating. He placed all of his energy and focus on a positive outcome, and Mia started to be more consistent with her eating and slowly gained weight.

The Law of Attraction is everywhere in our lives. The more you focus on the difficulty, the trouble, and the bad, the more of that you get. I know from an outside perspective that I can see just how much Mia had helped her foster dad to become a calm, convincing, confident leader who makes decisions fast. With his attitude, which you remember is made up of thoughts, feelings, and actions, he has become a great example of the type of leader you can be for your dog.

Mia was a huge challenge as far as dogs go, but she is now about 3 years old, a large female German Shepherd, and she does not have to endure the torture of a prong or shock collar. Her foster owner decided to keep her permanently, and now Mia shares his home with his other male German Shepherd. Likewise, her male companion dog shares in that same kindness. She is never given a command; she is only given gentle requests.

Mia's owner works very hard with these dogs each day to show he is a capable leader. Is it easy? No, but he has studied the method of Amichien Bonding and has my close guidance. He learns more and more every day about the importance of his feelings in a situation. He does not let the fact that he is a big guy get in the way of understanding just how he feels. He stays in tune to make sure a hard day at work is left there, and his focus on his way home is of a great dog eating her meal and being relaxed with her companion. Working with such a challenging dog pushes him to new limits, but he is meeting the challenge with great success. He also sees the benefit of having a relaxed presence that he feels on his way home to meet the dogs. He sees the results in Mia and has consequently become a better person.

Our foster dad in the above story took a big step when he made a decision to no longer worry about Mia's eating. The following quotes lead us into taking another step.

Learning to Take Risks

"If you let fear of consequence prevent you from following your deepest instinct, then your life will be safe, expedient, and thin."
– Katharine Butler Hathaway

"No one reaches a high position without daring."
– Publilius Syrus, Syrian-born Latin writer of maxims

We must live by our core beliefs, and for our canine friends, survival is one of them. When they ask, "What is in it for me"? it is often to be sure that they are safe. If you are looking at things through their eyes, you are able to see why the dog has such a strong need for a leader. If they risk their lives for the pack, they must fully trust the leader. Remember, however, that the leader is tested whenever there is a change. In the perspective of the pack, going on a hunt poses great risk. There may be a litter of pups left behind, or there may be rival packs nearby where the prey is often formidable. The trust and strength of the pack is paramount. With these great risks also come great rewards. They kill an elk and sustain no injury. They feed the pack and are at full strength to continue to survive.

When we take this ideology into our world, we don't focus on it as instinctually as a dog, but it is there and very strong. If you view objects through human eyes, then you understand why we have such a strong need for a leader. If we risk all we have for the family, company, or country, we must fully trust the leader. The leader will be tested whenever there is a change. In the perspective of the family, when going out to secure solid work, there may be a little one staying behind, or there may be large competition for the position and the corporate leaders are often just as formidable. The trust and strength of the family is paramount. With these great risks also come great rewards. You secure a position with a solid salary. Now you can feed the family and be at full strength, physically and emotionally to continue to survive.

I do not advocate taking foolish risks. I do not drive my car recklessly or do risky stunts to prove my courage, but taking risks goes together with fast decisions. Know the situation and make a good judgment about the outcome. If the pack is out on a hunt and the elk in the clearing is surrounded by another pack, the leader may decide to look elsewhere rather than take the risk of a fight with the other wolves. If there is only one other wolf stalking the elk, the risk makes more sense and the pack continues inward. Along the same idea, if there is a rival pack but the number of elk is high, the risk might be worth it as well. You need to look at the whole picture and make the decision, but remember to do it with confidence.

Whenever we need to make a decision, whenever we risk anything, we feel fear. Fear is fine, but you should never let it stop you from taking a risk. As a firefighter, I read the trade magazines about the happenings in the field. The following story exemplifies the risk our dogs take for us, and is a good lesson for us to learn about taking a risk.

After the September 11, 2001, terrorist attacks, humans were not the only heroes. The dogs upheld the spirit of gallantry as well. A New York City resident was on the 71st floor of the World Trade Center North Tower when the hijacked airliner struck the building

25 floors above him. The idea of escaping was only worsened by the fact he was blind. As his guide dog lay under his desk, the man unleashed him so the dog could escape. The guide dog was swept away as the mass of people fled the floor. He thought for sure he was going to die but hoped his dog could escape to safety. Despite the chaos and hysterical crowds, his dog returned and guided him down 70 flights of stairs, leading him to safety. This dog loved his owner so much that he was prepared to die with him. This exemplifies the risk dogs will take to protect their charges.

"Courage is being scared to death
but saddling up anyway."
– John Wayne

The definition of courage is not fearlessness, but feeling fear and doing it anyway. How many times have we heard of stories where dogs risk their lives for us? Guide dogs are not the only dogs that risk their lives for their owners. Every day family pets risk their lives to protect the ones they love. I remember reading one story about a Pit Bull Terrier named Chief who rescued a child and her grandmother from a cobra that slithered in the house through an open kitchen window. Chief became aware of the snake's presence and alerted the grandmother and child. As they stood terrified watching it spit venom and prepare to strike, Chief leapt between them and slammed the snake to the floor, only to suffer a mortal bite to the jaw.

These few stories show us that the risks in life are always present, but if we do not take them, then life cannot give us the rewards that hide behind those risks. Chief actually took a risk that cost him his life. It was done without hesitation. This is the extent dogs are willing to go for us.

We can also learn persistence from our dogs. To be truly successful, you must perfect the art of persistence. It is the most important mental strength to develop. The rewards that life has to offer may require risk to achieve, but you also need persistence to see your efforts pay off.

How do you develop persistence? First, you have to really want something. That want should be so strong that you make a decision. You decide deep down that you will achieve what you want. Then failure, rejection, even bankruptcy will not stop you from that goal.

"Lots of people limit their possibilities by giving up easily. Never tell yourself this is too much for me. It's no use. I can't go on. If you do you're licked, and by your own thinking, too. Keep believing and keep on keeping on."
– Norman Vincent Peale

PERSISTENCE

Persistence is defined as the ability to maintain action regardless of your feelings. Basically, you stick to your plan to achieve your goals even when you feel like quitting. No matter who you are or what your circumstances, at some point in your progress toward a goal your motivation will be tested. Sometimes you will feel motivated; sometimes you will not. Remember, however, that it is not your motivation that produces positive results. It is your actions. Accepting this fact will help you to alter your behaviors in order to maintain motivation. Persistence enables you to keep taking action even when you have lost your motivation. Therefore, you keep accumulating results.

Persistence also acts as a motivating factor. By continuing your actions no matter what, you will eventually get results and results, can be very motivating. It is important to note that persistence is not stubbornness. You develop persistence through self-discipline, which is the ability to take action regardless of your emotional state.

Imagine how your dog's life would change if you could harness the self-discipline to follow through on your goals no matter what. The goals you accomplish with self-discipline are unsurpassable. Self-discipline is one of the most important personal development tools that you need to develop, self-discipline empowers you to take charge of your life and better the life of your dog. It eliminates procrastination, disorder, and ignorance. It becomes a powerful force when combined with relinquishing old beliefs.

Remember earlier when I said that persistence is not stubbornness? So how do you know the difference? Start by asking yourself these questions:

Is your idea still something you want? If the answer is "no", then update your idea and move on. Otherwise you are simply being stubborn and are holding onto something you really don't want.

Is your goal still something you want? If not, update or abandon your goal. There is no need to hang on to a goal that no longer inspires you or fits in with your ever-improving life.

You beat resistance with persistence, not force or aggression. Many people lose their patience or become frustrated and resort to force or aggression. I am well aware of the patience it requires to deal with resistant dogs, especially those persistently resistant dogs. Dutchess was one of those dogs. Dutchess came to us by another rescue organization who could not deal with her barking. They tried all sorts of techniques to make her stop. I agreed to take her in as they know I can do wonders with dogs, simply because I understand their language. They could as well, if they only listened.

First, I changed her name. Since she was a black-and-tan coonhound, I decided to call her "Tilly-the Hunt-R". A 6-month-old that just wanted to be with people, she resisted that she had to live outdoors in the kennel area, she resisted that she needed to stay within the fence line of the property, that the bedroom garden was for a different group of dogs, that she needed to wear a collar. She was just like a typical 14-year-old girl doing her own thing and not following the rules. Tilly was the most persistent dog I have met in a long time. Her barking started the moment she heard anyone outside on any part of the 2.5 acres. I thank my neighbor for her acceptance of the situation.

Tilly's persistence eventually paid off. Tilly joined Scrappy as a kennel-mate, and the two got along just fine. Tilly's barking issue took a lot of learning on my part to get a handle on it. Persistence equals patience in my book. If they are persistent, you need patience. If you are persistent, then you gain patience and help them along the way. Ultimately, you help them you grow, and they in turn, help you. It is that simple. So if you do not have patience in the beginning, rest assured you will have it in the end. With patience and understanding, Tilly moved indoors, kept her collar on, responded to the recall, and learned that if she stayed within the boundaries of the garden, she would get a cuddle on the sofa after dinner. Tilly did find a great forever home, and I am now much more persistent and patient because of her. Persistence even after successive failures takes you where you want to go. You must have the vision, charged with enthusiasm! Worry never heals, prevents, or solves anything. Trust in you and do not let worry waste your time.

Standing your ground, taking risks, and all of this – along with the confidence you gained as a leader – allow you to make fast decisions that are always best for the pack.

Persistence Follows You Everywhere

How your dog behaves when you go off your property is indicative of how he sees you and will reflect more than almost anything else. It is a guide to exactly how much work you still have to do on the leadership front. Huskies recall beautifully for a convincing leader in exactly the same way as any other dog on the planet. Some breeders say that Terriers don't listen or you cannot do obedience with Chows. You might have heard that all Border Collies chase sheep or that Cocker Spaniels are aggressive. It is useful to know that different breeds have been carefully selected for certain characteristics, which means there are some inborn traits and tendencies. However with persistent effort, all of these dogs can be calm and relaxed and follow you willingly.

Persistence is a must for boarding kennels or shelters. When you apply the process of establishing leadership in the appropriate way, dogs wants to follow you and thus, you will have more adoptable dogs. You will have dogs that are relaxed when the owner picks them up, rather then stressed.

One of the most important things is consistency. The volunteers at the shelters can get so busy merely attending to a dog's physical needs that they forget to be consistent in the use of rules and signals. For dogs, these rules and signals are what help them to become more adoptable. Because, they understand more clearly their role, they relax. Through consistency with the protocol, dogs learn much quicker. If it is the correct protocol, then they learn good things.

In your life, persistence, consistency, and patience will pay off as well. How many Ph.D.'s, marriages saved. and injuries recovered are there from using these skills? You can thank your persistent dog for helping you achieve a skill that will get you far in life.

CHAPTER
–Six–

When Bad Things
Happen to Good Dogs

CHAPTER
-Six-

When I think of obsession, I think of a beautiful white shepherd mix named Uni. She spent seven months in an SPCA shelter where she suffered and was severely traumatized. When she came to me, she was a mass of insecurity and fear. Initially I noticed Uni's obsessive licking. Human nature made me feel sorry for her because she did it to appease and to show she meant no harm. This dog had been through a lot; there was definitely abuse in her past.

Once again, I gave her space and followed the reunite protocol. I was a calm, reassuring presence for her. Her needs were taken care of, and after a good bit of time, she settled down. When I called her to me for some appropriate affection, she rolled onto her back to show submission. I walked away as I was not going to reinforce that feeling in her. You see, her overly submissive actions meant that she wasn't in a happy mood. I gave her a minute and called her again. Usually the second or third time, she understood and would not roll over. This dog needed help. She needed to gain confidence in me and herself, and that would just take time. Within two days, I paired Uni with another rescue named Juno. He was her strength and she was his comfort. You will hear more of this pair as we continue.

Uni	Juno

For any dog with an obsession, you need to break the cycle. The best way is to interrupt it and give them calm reassurance by holding them in place, using a quiet, gentle freeze. Now, I do not mean cuddling, loving, or stroking them. I mean taking their collar while remaining calm and keeping them from continuing the obsessive behavior. This is done until the dog relaxes. It may take awhile in some dogs, but the time will get shorter and shorter.

The next dog I want to introduce you to is a great work in progress. She is still at the rescue as I am writing this book, as are the two from the previous story, Uni and Juno. These dogs need a very special owner to continue on with their care.

Sierra, "The Wild Child"

This beautiful dog has had no guidance whatsoever. She is like a child who has been locked in a room with no human contact. This stunning, blue-eyed little husky mix with a white fluffy coat obsessively jumped, nipped, and spun in circles, making it difficult to be around her.

How did I handle her? You guessed it, no eye contact, no speaking, and no physical contact except to push her off me. This dog had a lot of potential. Even though humans had given her no guidance, she still wanted to work on figuring us out. You cannot break through to a mind that is in such chaos. You must wait for an opening, a calm, to allow any learning to enter. Little by little, Sierra did just that. She slowly brought some of her chaos under control and in time, Sierra continues to relax and let the obsessions die.

Both Uni and Sierra had serious issues, as humans do when they are obsessed to a point that impacts their normal life. Through these dogs, I have learned to stop, breathe, focus on my goal, and take a step in that direction. If that step goes well, take the next step. If I start to falter, I relax and go back to the point where I got it right.

"I move forward in my life every day, even if it's only a tiny step, because I know that great things are accomplished with tiny moves, but nothing is accomplished by standing still."
– Zig Ziglar

The biggest item to be aware of is your "self". Know your faults, weaknesses, strengths, and good points. This is important because dogs will definitely test you. If, for example, your patience is low, then work to increase it while you work with the dogs. When you feel it faltering, stop the lesson, and do something else. Manage your weaknesses and work hard on your strengths. With my injured back, I learned to strengthen my good muscles and let them help support the weak ones.

When your mind is in a state of chaos as Sierra's was, no learning can occur. We need to recognize the times when our excitement gets the better of us and slow ourselves down, allow ourselves that awareness so our energy can stay positive. Chaotic energy is overpowering and highly negative. We want good vibrations to propel us forward. Be honest and know yourself. It is the only way we can grow.

Bad things often happen to good people and likewise to good dogs. Some are just given the wrong signals. and it causes them problems while others get into situations all on their own. Sometimes it has to do with their personality and sometimes their health creates an issue.

Remember Spanner? When we left the story in the beginning of the book. He had just begun his treatment of antibiotics and steroids but could not walk. By day two, he was up and greeting people at the door. Those steroids did an amazing job, and Spanner felt like a pup again. Spanner had several ups and downs, but the steroids and antibiotics always brought him back around. There were a few times I thought it was "time". But it never failed that when I began to think of putting him down, he would perk right up and act like a pup again. On one occasion, he did relapse, and I had to make a trip to the emergency room vet.

Once again, I was faced with a large financial estimate for testing. I looked at the old guy and told him I would do the tests if *he* felt good enough to give me another year. His quality of life was very important, and that would make the testing worthwhile. Mr. Spanner gave me a little over a year before I really knew it was time for me to let him go. His frailness made me realize that it was not fair to hold on. I arranged for the vet to come to the house. I brought Spanner out to the front yard, and he was given a sedative by the vet so he could be as comfortable as possible. He walked around the grass on that beautiful summer day, smelling the lawn for whatever his old nose would let him sense. I cooked a steak for him earlier, and he ate well. When the sedative took effect, he laid down. Then the vet gave Spanner the IV and the drugs, and it was over in seconds. It was very peaceful, but very sad as well.

Afterward, the other dogs walked into the yard and were given some time to smell him to know he was now gone. After so much work the last few months, with the daily incontinence and the falling, it was over. I knew it was the right thing to do, but I still cried because I already missed the old guy.

Spanner's energy transferred back to the universe, and I moved forward on my path to truly understanding dogs and gaining guidance from them. At the time, I did not think Spanner gave me anything but grief, but as life continued I learned that I had been mistaken. What a guy. I refer to him because he had so much to teach me. I could have been a much better owner to him now, but he fulfilled the purpose I attracted him for. What I can only do now is to help others, so then they can help their dogs, too.

Spanner was an old, stubborn dog. His life was tough, and by the time I took him in, he had lost patience for this species he was living with and became a grumpy old dog. He no longer even cared for his own kind. I know now that he saw himself as the leader and did not care if you followed him or not. He was done looking after the kids; he was going to be his own man. Spanner expected his food at a certain time, and after you gave it to him, you better leave the dining area. I did show him the proper signals as the leader and worked to show him I was not a threat with the food but rather the foodgiver. In time, even this old dog mellowed and the cats were finally safe to walk past him without losing a tuft of fur.

His awareness changed once he saw the right signals coming from me. Before it came time for Spanner's energy to move on, he was running and playing with the young dogs. He engaged me in some fun and frolic in the yard. His eyes sparked. Spanner was also able to take a treat from me and leave me with my fingers. He taught me to not judge a book by its cover. We cannot judge others by how they are at the moment we meet them. Circumstances can often interfere with a first impression. Before we make a final judgment, we need to get to know them. Work with them. Give them something and expect nothing in return. When I started the journey with Spanner, I did not see the great dog that laid within him. Now, I know differently. He was a terrific dog with a whole lot to teach me.

Dogs always manage to teach us something if we are willing to listen. These next two "kids" made a difference for Tracey Quigley and helped guide her to a better path in life.

GODZILLA'S STORY

In November 2003, I received an uncastrated 10-year-old Staffordshire Bull Terrier from RSPCA Bothwell Bridge Rescue Centre. The staff named him Godzilla because he was huge! Incidentally, he was the only dog that would not come out of the kennel; all I could see was a small pair of sad eyes at the back of the bedding. I gently called to him, but he would not budge. He was watching me but not making any move toward me. I had a feeling about this dog, so I sat down on the soaking wet concrete outside the metal fencing and just sat, not making eye contact, playing with my laces. It took about 15 minutes before he came out, head down, tail between his legs, and looking thoroughly sorry for himself.

The rescue staff explained he wasn't coping very well without company and was very depressed. I asked to see him in the playpen, and he was brought to me. What a difference when he was out of the kennel – tail up and wagging and very playful. He immediately rolled over in the wet to get his tummy scratched. It was love at first sight and I knew he was coming home with me. So I told the staff I would take him. All we had to do was complete the forms, and they said they would pop him back in the kennel well we fill in the paperwork. I protested at this point and said they could bring the paperwork outside because he was not going back into that kennel. They allowed him into the reception area where we completed the forms, and then we left to go home! Shortly afterwards, having tried several names, he responded to Tyson.

Later, I decided to get a female companion for Tyson. I took Tyson over to meet his new mate, and they got on wonderfully. I asked the owner to hold her for two weeks. Once the work was completed on my home, I went to pick her up and discovered she was limping badly. I took her to the vet that same week and was told she had broken her leg. The poor thing had to undergo an operation and recuperate for the next six to eight weeks. We had toileting trouble, but I knew it was due to the medication and her general condition.

The toileting and destructive behaviours were getting to be unbearable. The more I "trained her" (saying "No" while pointing to the pooh, etc.), the worse she got. I would come home after work to discover the drywall at the back door had been chewed badly. She had poohed and peed all over the living room, and destroyed the sofa and cushions. I had a bad day at work and thus, I lost my temper and smacked her rump, grabbed her by the scruff of the neck, and shoved her snout in the runny, stinking mess, screaming at her for being a bad dog. (I didn't understand separation anxiety and chewing at the time). Both Saph and Tyson cowered in their beds terrified of the ranting, lunatic human I had turned into. I cleaned up the mess, calmed down, and looked over at her cute face, and she tentatively slunk over to me with her tail down and licked my hand very submissively. Hating myself for what I had just done to this beautiful creature, I picked her up onto my lap, cuddled her, and cried and cried.

As much as I loved her I just couldn't take any more of her destructive behavior. I decided to find a new home for her, but I couldn't follow through on my decision. She had already had two previous homes. After reading Jan Fennell's book, I realized what this smart little dog had been trying to do – be an alpha and look after her baby. She was worried when I left her, so she chewed and messed in the house.

Unwittingly, I gave her a job she couldn't do, in a world she didn't understand, and then I shouted at her for doing the job to the best of her ability. I actually cried as I read Jan's book, for it had become clear what had been happening with Saph. When I look back on Saph's behavior now, I have the greatest respect and admiration for that dog, because she would not give up her status even when I got angry. If anything, she tried harder. She is a smart dog. Once I understood Amichien Bonding, it took my relationship with my dogs to a whole new level of understanding. The subtleties of their signals amazed me, as did the power of a simple gesture like eye contact.

I have come to the conclusion that dogs are intelligent animals that have important needs similar to our own, and it's no wonder they are referred to as man's best friend. If everyone would appreciate his dog's "wolf behavior-instinct" then we would treat our pets better than we treat our own best friends. I decided that I would love to do Jan's work and help other like-minded owners' love and respect their dogs. All three of us have found happiness. We've had our good times and bad, but thanks to Jan and her Amichien Bonding, our time together now is for the most part stress-free and great.

Tracey Quigley, Scotland
www.pawsandthinkdoglisteners.co.uk

Jacqui Murk felt the experience of Basher was an important lesson to herself and others, as well. Aggression is difficult to handle if you are not aware of the canine language. Not all dogs that growl and bite are bad dogs. In fact, most are just confused by our actions.

Basher's Story

Eileen contacted me because her Yorkshire Terrier, Basher, was very aggressive during grooming. Basher was 9 years old and wouldn't be sedated by a vet while grooming. Eileen couldn't wipe Basher's eyes because he showed such aggression; he even tried to bite Eileen. As I was explaining the Amichien Bonding method to Elaine, Basher jumped on the sofa. I told Eileen to put him on the floor. After this, he showed his teeth. I then told Eileen that we would leave the living room and go into the hallway, so that he would lose the pack because of his behavior. After awhile, we returned to the living room and I continued my explanation of the method.

Eileen showed me how Basher reacted when she would get a tissue out of her pocket to wipe his eyes. He started to growl and showed his teeth. Eileen recently lost her husband after a long battle with illness. During that period, she nursed her husband. Since his death, she had put all her love toward Basher. I explained to her that Basher feels the need to protect her, that he is very alpha.

After four days, Eileen contacted me because Basher ignored her for about 24 hours, he didn't want to come to her. She was in tears on the phone. I explained to her to stick it out and that Basher will give in and it will go better from then on.

After six days, Eileen phoned me that she can now clean Basher's eyes with a tissue. He just let her do it. She was very happy with this. She made an appointment with the groomer to clip his nails.

I phoned her after 10 days and she told me that everything went okay with the groomer. No aggression at all. Basher was very calm. Eileen was very happy with the result.

Jacqueline Murk, Ireland
Dog Listener

Not all nasty dogs need to stay this way. There is always a reason. It usually revolves around a miscommunication. Eileen wanted to give all that extra love to Basher after she lost her husband, but what came across to Basher was that Eileen was not capable to make the decisions for their pack. So he became nasty and aggressive. This is the way some dogs react to taking on the decision-making role. No harm, no foul in this situation, but many dogs are killed every year simply because we do not speak their language. Many relationships end because two people cannot communicate with each other. People of different beliefs and religions fight wars because they cannot speak to one another. Species are destroyed because one cannot understand the other. This is a lesson for us in just how much breaking through this language barrier with our dogs can do for the relationship.

Nasty dogs are a good example of what frustration can do. When you cannot communicate with someone and you let frustration settle in, you can tend to be snappy toward others. If we use the example set by this specific personality type of dog and choose not to be that type of human, we can take control of how we feel. We no longer let the situation control our feelings. When you run across those snappy people who are frustrated and take it out on you, know that you are in control of how you feel. Smile and make the decision to feel good, have the right action, and choose your thoughts wisely. This keeps your attitude in the right place to attract the things you want and keeps you in control of your feelings.

As we move into taking responsibility, let me share the next few stories with you. For me, these are difficult stories. The outcomes had hard lessons to learn. That is what happens in life sometimes, and we need to use it to propel ourselves forward. Many people let these tough lessons get them down, some even quit. We have to remember that persistence in life is also important, and your goal is what you should keep focused on.

CRYSTAL'S STORY

"Boy, does she have a whole lot of energy", is exactly what I thought when I first met Crystal. A little Terrier mix about 10 weeks old, she was not even 10 pounds. This was a little bundle I refer to as "a keeper". I knew I needed to find her a home, but I was enjoying the time she was with me. She would curl up in bed next to me and sleep. She never let her size interfere in her play with the big dogs. She gave the big lab puppy, Little Bear, a good run for his money. She jumped right over him and ran under his legs – almost knocking him over at times because he didn't know which way to look. These two made a great pair.

One Friday afternoon, I noticed something was wrong. Crystal came in from playing in the yard and vomited. I did not get too concerned because dogs occasionally did this, but it seemed odd so I kept my eye, on her. I called the vet the next day when I saw her throw up several more times. Each time was bile, and she was getting lethargic. At first, I thought it might have been plant toxicity. I noticed a pod in the garden that had been played with, and I grew concerned that Crystal might have swallowed something toxic. The vet told me what to do and said to monitor her. She had a very rough night, and Sunday morning I shot off to the Emergency Vet to see what was going on. Crystal also started to experience bloody diarrhea. I was almost certain it was not Parvo, but of course that was the first thing we checked for. The vet even ran a second test to rule out a false negative. It was not Parvo. I told them of my suspicion of plant toxicity and so we did a pretty in-depth blood screening. It came back with serious liver failure, most likely due to a Sago Palm nut. The pod I saw would not do damage to the liver. I had never seen any sago nuts in the garden, but it did not really matter. The damage was done, and it was irreversible.

Crystal was given IV fluids and kept stable and resting while I did my own fast research. I had five Reiki practitioners working on her by sending healing thoughts. We thought we might have a shot at things if we could get some improvement in a few hours of fluid therapy. We never even got a few hours as her little body gave out. What on earth could be so important to teach me that this little life had to go so soon?

I hate when I have to learn some lesson revolving around death. It was not a case of my causing her death, but I still feel responsible. You do your best to watch them, but just like kids, they can always get into something no matter how cautious you are.

Crystal

Recently, TV talk show host Oprah Winfrey lost one of her beloved dogs to a tragic accident. Oprah wrote for her *O Magazine* readers how she felt as though she had been stabbed in the chest. Her dog Gracie's death really shook her.

Gracie was the smallest of Oprah's Golden Retrievers and recently turned 2 years old. She choked to death on a plastic ball that was in the grass. It was not the usual practice to allow the dogs to have those balls, but like we so often learn, things have a way of finding themselves inside our dogs' mouths.

Oprah had left the dogs under the supervision of the dog walker for only 20 minutes. She received the call and immediately ran out to the location to find her Gracie and the caretakers performing CPR. It was too late, though, Gracie was dead. She choked on the ball. This was a most horrible accident, but Oprah did not believe in accidents. She stated, "I know for sure that everything in life happens to help us live".

Through her grief, she asked her dear Gracie what she was here to teach her that only death could show her. Gracie had been full of life, constantly running and chasing squirrels. Oprah often told her, *"Gracie, slow down"*. She would always be calling after her, *"Graaacie, come!"*.

The day after the tragic event, Oprah called Gracie once more. This time she did not come, and Oprah realized how much pleasure she had taken in calling for her. Through a lot of tears, she realized Gracie's life was a gift to her, but her death was an even greater one.

Just prior to her beloved dog's death, Oprah had a physical and was advised to take some time off. She had been going too hard for too long and had forgotten to take time for herself. When her doctor called, she confessed that she had so many meetings on the list but had not scheduled one for herself.

The next day Gracie died.

Slow down, you are moving too fast. Oprah got the message. "Thank you for being my saving Gracie."

This story is close to my heart because I understand exactly what Oprah went through. Similarly, my schedule had gotten very hectic, and I was running quickly from one task to the next. It was my responsibility to deal with the projects I had chosen to undertake, and I accepted that. But I had to remember to take time and enjoy the process of what I was doing.

TAKING RESPONSIBILITY FOR YOUR LIFE

What are your feelings as you recall the events and circumstances in your life? Do you feel successful, happy, unworthy? No matter the emotions, you must first accept responsibility for them. You and only you are responsible for your feelings, actions, and ultimately your life. Life does not just happen. Once we can acknowledge this fact, we can create the life we have always wanted. A short time after Crystal died, Juno and Uni had an encounter that ended tragically as well. This lesson was also a hard one to learn because it was my fault. I just wish it were a lesson I could have learned by having a close call instead of a death.

Each morning I let the adoptable dogs out to potty, and Juno and Uni went into the cottage garden. While they were there, I took one of the puppies out front on lead for her potty, and quickly returned to supervise the two white fluff balls. Well, the pup had just finished her business when I heard a squawk! I rushed into the back garden and into the screened-in pool area to see Uni and Juno chasing Socs, the blue-and-gold macaw, out from the patio. I yelled and they called off the chase. I immediately scooped up Socs and quickly looked him over to see if he had been injured. Nothing looked wrong, but in seconds I knew that was not the case. My extensive training in different areas of animal rescue taught me about something referred to as a "capture syndrome". In about 30 seconds, Socs looked up at me as I cradled him in my arms and then lowered his head and died.

Even though the dogs had not physically injured him, his system could not handle the immediate rush of adrenaline. Basically, he had a heart attack from shock. I was beside myself. Immediate

143

anger poured over me. I wanted those dogs out of my sight. I cried, I paced, and I held him. What happened was that in my rush to let an earlier group of dogs out from the main house, I forgot to close the patio door. The house dogs always go out to the garden through the patio, past the birds. The dogs have never had any concern for the birds, only for bird seeds they could scavenge off the floor.

Socs was also raised with St. Bernards and was used to dogs being around and near him. He was also the only bird to have free access to the top of his cage via an open cage door. He sat on the top rail of his door. I let Juno and Uni, the culprits, out on the opposite side of the patio. They managed to squeeze under a weak spot in the fence and slip through a rip in the screened-in pool enclosure. This gave them easy access to the patio, since the sliding door was open. I always close that door. This one time I forgot. *One time* was all it took. It was not even five minutes that the dogs were unattended. It was only a few seconds before I got there after I heard the squawk. The squawk was probably when one of the dogs put its paws up on the cage to see what was on top. When the door started to swing closed, Socs probably fell and squawked as that happened. He more than likely took off to get out of the scene, with two dogs close behind. These dogs are not aggressive, nor were they at that moment. They just saw something that looked neat to play with. It just happened to be a poor choice of play toy.

Now, I might take a lot of flak for this story and people might think I was horribly irresponsible, but believe me, that is not the case. I know how quickly accidents happen. I was a firefighter and that was our job security – accidents! I do know that complacency kills and in this case, I learned to slow down and make sure step one is complete before moving on to step two. This was not a complacent thing, it was, "I'm doing my best, but I slipped up". I have a quote from an associate named Rita that sums it up, "When you make a mistake, don't beat yourself up but rather look for the lesson. It is there. Failure breeds success in all you do, in everything you do."

Take time with whatever you are doing. Enjoy it! It does not matter how late you are or how behind you are. It does not matter how much you have to do. Smile and be grateful for that moment. Each activity you do should get your *full* attention. Each person, animal, project, mission should be your focus when you are in that moment. Make sure you finish what you are doing before you move on. I know you can multi-task, but make sure the current interest is safely put away before passing GO and collecting $200. Each time you leave someone could be the last time you ever see them. Make sure you are ready to leave them for that very reason. I am not saying to project doom and gloom, I am saying to rejoice and be happy with them and let them know it. We are talking about good vibrations. And when someone does leave us, it is okay to be sad.

It is okay to grieve. Realize they are gone but their energy has simply moved on into another form. Energy is never created nor destroyed. It moves into form and through form and back into form. Remember the chapter on the universal laws.

Take solace that the depth of your grief is a mirror to the love that you felt. The poem *The Mirror of Death* by John Stevens is a beautiful piece. John describes the death of a beloved dog that has left a gaping hole that was once filled with love. "Days of grief immediately followed. Friends tried to say the right words. Hugs were given generously. Everything helped, but they couldn't fill the void in my soul. I tried pep talks to convince myself that it was all for the best and so on and so on. I missed my dog and that was it."

John goes on to describe how while walking past a store he noticed his reflection in the window and it then made sense to him. "Like the reflection in a mirror or glass, death is the reflection of life. The greater the love you felt, the greater the grief. There are people who die every day that I feel no grief for. My dear Sarah's death created a deep and profound sorrow. However, it was only so deep and profound because our love for each other had been so deep and profound, too. The sorrow was a mere reflection of the joy we shared."

If you are in a similar situation, make the decision to start to feel good. Take actions to make that happen and do not let sadness hold you down or pull you into depression. Celebrate the time you had, or the experience you shared, and be glad for the opportunity. Grieve for what you miss but embrace what will come.

So to honor those wonderful little beings that have come into my life for a reason, I celebrate you, I miss you, I have learned from you. You were all very special, thank you: *Balto, Neffie, Karma, Chulo, Socs, Crystal, Iggy, Ro-J, Lilly, Lil'lovebird, PJ, Spats, Shasta, Tony, Bacall, Bogey, Cleo, LilMan, Scooter, Draco, Lady, Tude, Casey, Isabeau, Spanner, Moses, Casper, Phoenix.* In 39 years of life I have had a lot of time to see many go and I know I must work through others that will go as well.

CHAPTER
–Seven–

I Know How You Feel...

CHAPTER
– *Seven* –

If you believe you are superior to a dog, then you have no respect for them. When you have respect for your dog, your dog will give you everything it can to enjoy life and to help you learn about the wonders of this earth. Our dogs have feelings, and to disrespect that with harsh training or aversive methods is the same as abuse in the eyes of nature. Dogs do not hide how they feel about you. You know right from the start if you are considered a friend or a foe. Animals do show emotions – such as fear, anger, sadness, surprise, and joy, to name a few. Knowing this should change the way we deal with them. For this reason, we should put more effort into treating them the right way and not allowing abuse to occur, especially in the name of training.

These first few stories will give you some great examples of just how important feelings are to your dog. Some super-sensitive dogs even cause you to reach down even further to check what is going on with your own feelings. These dogs are some of the most frustrating ones to deal with. That is another lesson they give you. Dogs are full of lessons for us humans. It is only a case of "us humans" actually listening for that lesson.

Brandy comes to mind the second you use a word such as "sensitive". I first heard about her when her owner, Sharon, called. Sharon did not know what to do with this dog. She recently adopted her, and the transition was not going too well. Brandy was a cowering mess. She could not be kept in a crate because the separation anxiety was too high. She could not deal with being alone. The dog tore up the doorway molding, the carpet at the door, the tack strips that hold the carpet down, the window treatments, cushions, and curtains. Sharon tried everything she could. She hired a traditional trainer as well as a behaviorist to work with Brandy, before finally resorting to putting her on medication.

It is amazing to me that people try everything before someone gives them "the book", or tells them about what we do. It is that wonderful Law of Attraction at work to bring people help when they are at the point of being able to accept it. I went to see Sharon and Brandy, and explained what the dog needed from her and gave her the tools to do it. Sharon learned the canine language and Brandy's behavior improved. They made great progress, and Brandy was no longer tearing things up when left alone. There was still the issue of separation anxiety during a storm, so I continued to work with the two. It was very important for Sharon to fully understand what her dog was going through and why. Sharon needed to realize the severity of the situation from Brandy's point of view. Right from the start, Brandy saw that Sharon needed to be cared for. The dog took the leadership role and was totally unqualified for it. Sharon implemented the method, but she had a few "chinks" in her armor.

When I went back the second time to get more information from Sharon, I realized another factor in the situation. Brandy was one of those super-sensitive dogs you do not often see. Sharon admitted she was concerned about Brandy when she was out. She said she constantly worried about what would happen if a storm arose. Sharon gave off the vibrations and the feelings of the exact thing she did not want. Her focus was not on what she did want, but rather on what she feared. More damage, more issues. After realizing this, she confessed that she, too, was slightly uncomfortable with storms. This was a huge breakthrough for us in defining Sharon's leadership role. If Sharon wanted to be viewed as the leader for this highly sensitive dog, she needed to be the leader in her head, in her heart, in her thoughts, and in her feelings. Most importantly, she needed to leave the frustration at the door.

A sensitive dog, or any dog for that matter, instinctively picks up on the slightest frustration of their owners. That frustration translates to the dog as something bad or weak, and they perceive their owner to have weak leadership skills. Sharon is working on improving her feelings and attracting what she wants. Her dog is a perfect sensor for Sharon to know how truly calm and relaxed, and how happy and in control, she really is.

Another highly sensitive dog I have had the pleasure to know and live with for a few weeks was Ella. What a wonderful dog, but a real handful, too. I need to give her a lot of credit for getting me to an even higher place with my understanding of the dog-human bond, as well as the inner feelings that most people do not ever connect with.

My clients lived out of state, so we made arrangements to fly me in so I could have a day to "arm" them against this little 6-month-old Labradoodle. From the time Ella was about 4 months old, she was quite the nipper. She went off on a tangent and would do drive-by "nip and run" attacks. Hard to believe that this little 15-pound sweetheart delivered a bite with such fury. She constantly jumped on the owners, as well as guests, and frequently pawed the counter to see what might be there to eat.

When I arrived at my clients' home Ella jumped on me, but I calmly walked past her and gave a slight push off. I did the typical reunite protocol, but Ella was a most persistent jumper. After a second jumping attempt, with the same light push off, came a third. At that point, while ignoring her, I guided her out to an area away from the pack. I came back and explained the canine language to her soon-to-be new leaders. With her jumping, Ella could have easily fit into the chapter on persistence, but her real lessons to us were yet to come. A few hours into our consultation, Ella settled down and rested quietly. My clients were amazed because with past visitors she was always "in their faces". This was a great sign that she was picking up on my communication. By the end of the trip, the new leaders were ready to go the distance to show Ella they could do the job. I left and had two new friends, whom I thoroughly enjoyed spending a day with and looked forward to hearing about their progress.

Things did improve, but like anyone who had been challenged for their position, Ella was not going to give up easily. After several nipping incidents, one of which broke the skin, my client considered returning the dog to the breeder. She felt she was not capable of giving the dog what she needed. We were able to coordinate to get Ella to my place for a few weeks. This separation gave me some one-on-one time with Ella, as well as time for my client to heal physically and mentally and enabling her to become the calm, convincing, confident leader that Ella was going to need. I personally worked to show Ella that this type of behavior was inappropriate.

It was not until the 10-day point that Ella became comfortable enough to test my leadership skills. She initiated a drive-by nip attack that resulted in no reaction from me and so it stopped. The next time the challenge was on. Ella was outside with a young lab named Lil'Bear and me. When the charge came at me and I did not react, Lil'Bear took it upon himself to welcome Ella to a game. He performed the customary puppy play bow and Ella decided he would do just fine to continue the drive-by game. As Ella flew by Lil'Bear, he spun on his hind side, not knowing what to do. I stood back and watched, amused.

One lesson I learned about Ella was that if you had *any* reaction or rise in your feelings when she initiated the drive-by nip, it would be difficult to stop. She was just like one of those annoying people who poke their finger at you and if it bothers you, they do it again. But if they do not get a rise out of you, it is no fun and they stop. I predicted when Ella was getting ready for the game. You could see the buildup of energy.

As I progressed in remedying the drive-by nip behavior, I learned more about Ella and her challenges. She was a very subtle dog. Even when she was an "over-the-top" jumper, it was so dainty you hardly knew she was on you. She tested your skills in other areas, too.

I arrived home one afternoon and led the dogs out back to use the bathroom. Ella stood at the end of the sofa and would not follow. I was in a hurry, so I called to her, "Let's go potty". She would not move. I needed the dogs to go out right away because I had to leave again for another few hours. I went to Ella without making eye contact or further verbal contact, and gently guided her outside. After returning home again and following the same pattern to let the dogs out, Ella still would not come. I called her to come potty. Yet again she would not move. I realized I was still in a bit of a fluster from the quick coming and goings of that day, so I stood and took a deep breath and let everything go. I released the tension from the day and felt more at ease. I called Ella again, and this time she immediately came to me, and out she went with the rest of the pack.

Now, I was not in the least bit angry or frustrated with Ella. But it did not matter to her, it only mattered that my feelings were not right. Anger and frustration are both negative feelings. Even though my voice conveyed a gentle tone, what was going on inside was vastly different. This led me to stumble onto something truly amazing. I know how important it is to be calm for our dogs. I know how important it is to have the attitude of the leader. What I never experienced was to what depth it meant to be calm and have the right attitude. Some dogs are fine when your inner feelings are still a bit frazzled by your normal life. They still challenge you because that is their natural way, but dogs that are super-sensitive to feelings challenge you as the leader far more than usual when they sense something negative. They also need to be convinced more thoroughly of your capabilities as a leader before they fully relinquish control to you. Sensitive dogs bring you to a better understanding of yourself because they will make you take a deep look inside at those feelings you may not be paying any attention to at all. This helps you greatly in your growth process and attracting what you want in life.

Ella taught me that I, too, am super-sensitive to other people's feelings. If someone is frustrated or angry at something else when they are communicating with me, I do not like that feeling that I get from them. I would much rather prefer they let that feeling go and deal with me while they are experiencing good positive feelings.

Many people are in awe at the sensitivity and healing capabilities of the dog. How many heads can you count that turn to look as they see a service dog go by? These dogs usually wear identifying capes that remind people that the dog is working and not to pet them. If they did not do this, it would take the owner hours to make it to their destination, because people would constantly stop and want to pet the dog. We are drawn to them. If you are ever in a hospital when the therapy dog arrives, you will see all the children immediately perk up at a chance to pet and show love to their most welcome visitor. These dogs have a strong sensitivity to those who need them most. The person can even be unconscious and the monitors will relay a calmer signal. Dogs can be highly in tune to our feelings, and we should be honored that they respect and love us so much.

Animal emotions and empathy have value in their own right but also in their importance to human well-being. Humans need animals, and dogs are drawn to our emotions. We share and understand our emotions which enable us to form deep, long-lasting bonds with animals. There have been studies involving hospitalized heart patients that prove the benefit of these bonds. A patient who had a visit from a dog experienced decreased anxiety more than those who did not. This next story shows the level of emotion and sensitivity dogs can have for their human companions. Sandy shares the story of Mom and Ruffles.

MOTHER, YOU NEED A DOG

Edith & Ruffles

Knowing I'd join the world of work after college, it was evident that with me gone my mother needed a companion. In 1976, my sister, mother, and I traveled up river to Norwich, Connecticut. Our purpose was to look at a family of salt-and-pepper Miniature Schnauzers.

Our research of breeders had led us here. When we arrived, I stepped out of the car and a blur of nine funny bodies flew by (well only four to be exact) followed shortly by one fast, definitely in-charge puppy. As we watched, she put all of the others under the truck. She then turned facing us and came running over. Our eyes met and the contract was sealed. All the way home hugs and kisses were shared by all. Mother had a dog.

Having had miniature Manchesters and Chihuahuas growing up, we wanted something stronger and medium-sized, as well as easy to handle. Yeah, right!

Countess Misty Ruffles was a home-spoiled, run-of-the-house, Queen of All. Much joy and comfort and unbelievable humor filled my mother's life. For nine years, they were home and travel buddies.

When my mother's cancer became debilitating, we made plans to fly her to Connecticut and then I'd drive up. As we put her bags in the van, Ruffles ran out the door and jumped up onto my mother's lap. Mom gave her a hug and told her to wait. I took her back into the house explaining as I went that she and I were going to drive. The connection was there for sure – her person was leaving her and this was not a good thing.

Two days later, we arrived in Connecticut. Mom and Ruffles were together again and they slept close. The next morning after breakfast in my mother's room, she asked where Ruffles was. I told her, "Sleeping right next to you". She patted her, smiled at me, and was gone. We all gathered in the room holding hands in the family circle. Without a moment's hesitation, a low, slow howl developed from the small gray figure on the floor inside the circle. Her head extended into the air with long vocal wails. Some people have heard this cry, but to witness that moment was unforgettable!

Ruffles then came to live with me and together we shared the loss. The time came for me to start teaching school again, and I'd have 14 days of Band Camp. My friend Nancy, who had several dogs, agreed to keep Ruffles for me. This would be her first time ever in a crate. When I came home Ruffles had learned to love her crate as a safe haven and also had learned how to be part of a pack. Yes, dogs let you live with them, but I've learned I should be the leader.

Thank you Nancy Fishinger, my dog buddy, for introducing me to many wonderful dogs and for taking Ruffles and me one step further. And thank you, Ruffles for making our mother's passing as pleasant as possible. You knew how important it was to be with her, especially in the end, and of course you were.

Sandy Smith, Montverde, Florida
www.ladyofjustice.biz

I find the story of Ruffles very touching. The bond that the dog had with Sandy's mother was very special. It must have been quite comforting for her mother in those last minutes to know her dog was right by her side. Ruffles' howl is a great example of our animal companions feeling and expressing emotion as well.

Not all dogs have a deep sensitivity, which is why not all dogs can do work in a therapy setting. Personality also plays a role, but with a sensitive dog, you must have a calm demeanor. These dogs can be traumatized if led by a strong hand, and really there is no need to when you can convey the right message to them in a kind way that they understand.

In the working dog world, those sensitivities need to be taken into account. The search-and-rescue dogs that work tirelessly at the scene of a disaster need to be given special care to keep their spirits up.

Hundreds of search-and-rescue dogs and their handlers worked at the site of the September 11, 2001, World Trade Center collapse. Footpad lacerations, eye irritation, dehydration, and heat stroke were among the many problems the veterinary medical personnel were trained and prepared to treat. But they were unprepared to treat canine depression. This occurs when eager dogs find too few living survivors in the rubble. These dogs are trained to find live people. It is positive energy for them, but they only found cadavers and body parts. But the handlers tried to stay upbeat, because the dogs took cues from them. The handlers had a difficult task since everyone was very upset. Eventually, the dogs received affection, which improved their morale considerably.

The job of the search dogs in these situations shows another example of the emotions they share with us. Their sensitivity to the environment they are working in makes them susceptible to depression, just like humans. Animal suffering is very real and must be addressed to keep them healthy and happy. It is beneficial to the dogs for the handlers to keep the most positive feelings and also to remain calm and confident. When the handler needs to be alone to deal with their own emotions, they should find a place away from the dogs and take the time to address those difficult feelings. This is the same for you or me in our emotional times.

Dogs already familiar with assisting people with emotional issues are still going to seek a leader in their pack. If the dog is actually living alone with the person who needs emotional support, the proper signals will be a key factor to having the dog stay relaxed and stress-free. It is important to have just the right type of personality in that dog, otherwise you will have a dog that challenges you often as they sense the weakness.

Often, when someone has an issue with depression or anxiety, having to reach down and find the strength to help your dog or another person can be the factor to pull you out of that situation. As a big believer in natural healing and using aspects of Eastern medicine, when I was suffering from PTSD and depression, medication for me was not an option. Animals helped me to keep going on days when my anxiety or depression was high. Losing a career I wanted so badly was a difficult thing for me to deal with. Even though I was working with the animals that I loved so much, I felt like I failed myself. I felt like I gave up, I should have been able to rehabilitate myself and get back to my firefighting career.

It was only later with the help of my dogs that I could see this was not true at all. I had to be strong for them. Weakness in the pack is not tolerated. That is why some dogs will all of a sudden attack an older dog. They are attempting to force them out of the pack. It is up to us to keep that older pack member safe. It is also up to us to be sensitive to the needs of others and aware of the fact that our lessons in life are not always easy ones. My vibrations changed the more I became aware of just how important feelings really are in our lives and the lives around us. I no longer focused on pain, depression, and weakness. I began to find my strength again and did things to feel good. My attitude changed. Through this new thinking and feeling, I conquered my issues and kept them under control. The dogs were a big part of that.

I have a huge soft spot for Pit Bulls since many great ones have crossed my path. These next two service dogs had the right personality but started off facing a whole lot of prejudice.

ANNIE AND KOTA'S STORY

Annie was 4 months old when she was rescued from a shelter. The fact that she was a Pit Bull usually meant an early death due to the prejudice against the breed, but luckily it did not happen. She had good aptitude for work, so it was decided that she should be trained to be a search dog. She soon met young Kota. She and Kota were inseparable, so as soon as possible Kota was trained as a search dog, too.

Kota and Annie's training took many months, but soon they were ready to join an organization. Of course what happened next can often be expected when you have Pit Bulls. They were told they were not welcome. After some debate, it was decided the two could join the group. The problem was that no one wanted to work their dogs along with the two Pit Bulls. Almost a year went by and it was time for evaluation. After their perfect performances, one of the evaluators allowed the dogs to play with her dog. From then on, everyone accepted both Pit Bulls.

Annie and Kota absolutely loved people, so to compliment their training they went into therapy work as well. When the woman answering the phone found out that Annie and Kota were Pit Bulls, she ended the conversation. Once again, there was going to be breed prejudice against the two. Sticking with it, another phone call was made two weeks later. When asked what kind of dogs they were, the answer was, "Terriers and they also do search and rescue". That seemed to do the trick! A couple of months later, Annie and Kota went to the rehab center for patient evaluation. The organizer waited in the lobby, and she was not pleased to see two Pit Bulls. But to the organizer's dismay, a child sitting in the lobby ran up to Annie and started petting her. Then a man in a wheelchair came by and asked if he could pet the dogs. Everyone was happy to see the dogs.

The organizer said, "You know, I learned something today. I guess Pit Bulls aren't all bad. Here is a list of hospitals, rehab centers, and convalescent homes that could sure use your help. Good job."

Many people wonder why owners do therapy work and search and rescue with their dogs. It is just the continuation of the deep connection we have with this species. Those dogs that have the aptitude and personality find a joy in helping, they have that special sensitivity to reach people, and it truly does not matter what breed the dog is.

In the 2006 *Handbook on Animal-Assisted Therapy*, researchers Chia-Chun Tsai and Erika Friedmann acknowledge that the research is far from definitive; however, studies have found that dogs can reduce loneliness, lower anxiety, and give a smile to the depressed. I can personally attest to how the animals helped me through my depression and kept me going. However, leadership and behavior problems can arise in a dog that senses your weakness in these areas.

Dogs are also a great part of helping young boys with sensitivity and caring. Our society often teaches a boy that emotions are a sign of weakness. In a 2003 paper in the journal *American Behavioral Scientist,* Alan Beck, Sc.D., Director of the Center for the Human-Animal Bond at Purdue University's School of Veterinary Medicine, and Aaron H. Katcher, M.D., a psychiatrist at the University of Pennsylvania, make the point that our culture has few forms of play that mold caring and nurturing behaviors in male children. "Boy children", says Beck, "tend to be very self-conscious about having to take care of younger brothers and sisters. They don't play tea party or dollhouse, because that's Mommy stuff. However, taking care of an animal is a notable exception. Caring for your dog is always okay."

*"Because humans and dogs evolved together
I believe we share certain patterns of thought
that allow us to live together."*
– Vilmos Csányi

Csányi suggests that dogs perceive when a person or another animal is in danger (hence the ability of wolves to prey on the weak of a herd, or the dog to detect cancer or seizures) and can empathize with the emotional state of people who are sad or ill. Marc Bekoff, the author of *The Emotional Lives of Animals*, agrees. He recounts the story of a dog that saved the life of his canine companion by awakening their owner to let him know that the second dog was ill. Bekoff also tells a tale about his own dog, Jethro, who adopted an orphaned rabbit and, years later, rescued an injured bird. "I think Jethro is a truly compassionate soul", writes Bekoff. "He could easily have gulped each down with little effort. But you don't do that to friends, do you?"

Bravo felt the same way about Bart. In the story of Black Bart, Jane Osinski shows us the lengths that some animals will go to for their friends.

BLACK BART

Black Bart was a rat. In screen life, he was a western outlaw. In our home, he was a real rat. Dogs, cats, and people usually hate rats.

I would have set a trap for him, but a mouse once saved our air conditioner and I promised then never to set another trap. So, when we first discovered Bart, I could not bring myself to trap him. Besides, I thought my dog or cat would dispatch him for me.

Instead, my chow, Bravo, and our cat, Patches, thought Bart was Mistletoe, a pygmy hamster we once had. Bravo carried his food in his mouth, distributing it where Bart could feast on it. Patches pushed her food off the table. They enhanced their relationship through sharing. Not satisfied with the variety, Bart chewed through the plastic food containers and helped himself.

In an effort to conserve on pet food, Peggy, a friend of mine, set a glue trap. Bart evaded it for several forays, but one day his tail got caught. Squeaking all the way, he headed for his hole. Peggy darted after him, only to be stalled by Bravo's body. Bravo witnessed the commotion and decided to intervene on behalf of his friend. Bart managed to leave the trap behind at the entrance of his hole. With his friend's help, he made an escape.

Bart developed other food tastes. He honed in on my chocolate cache. Ignoring all the other candies laying around, he stole every one of *my Snickers bars. But he did not get credit at first. I thought my friends and family had developed a taste for my treats.*

At Christmas, when I set the table for dinner, I discovered Bart's secret. He stashed every Snickers in an out-of-the-way corner, one tooth mark in each candy. Apparently, Bravo and Patches did not believe in snitching, either, because I remembered seeing Bravo sniff that area often.

I seriously considered ignoring my promise to not set traps. However, Bravo and Patches' loyalty to their friend was what brought reconsideration.

Bravo and his pal Patches demonstrated a lot about keeping relationships alive. They truly showed patience, tolerance, and loyalty. They were willing to overlook appearances, and the biggie, they were willing to share. I suppose if they could do that, then I could too and just learn to live with a few less Snickers bars to boot.

Jane M.D. Osinski, Orlando, Florida
Author

Dogs never cease to amaze me. I know I have seen pictures of a female dog nursing kittens before, but befriending a rat or a rabbit or even a bird is a new one to me. We find something to learn in every situation. We can also see the bond, the love that can develop in the animal world.

Jeffrey Moussaieff Masson, author of *Dogs Never Lie about Love*, has no doubt that dogs empathize with humans. "If they're not self-aware, how come they can appear so guilty?" he asks. Csányi even goes so far as to compare canine attachment with human love.

Masson believes dogs could teach us a thing or two about love and, indeed, may already have done so. Dogs have been part of our evolutionary environment, just as we have been part of theirs. "There may be mutual influences", he says.

Jim and Jamie Dutcher understand the love that is shared among the pack. They recounted the grief and mourning after the loss of Motaki. She was an omega (lowest rank) female wolf in the Sawtooth pack. Motaki was killed by a mountain lion. "The pack lost their spirit and playfulness. They no longer howled as a group, but rather sang alone in slow mournful cries. They were depressed. Their tails and heads were held low, and they walked softly and slowly when they came upon the place where Motaki was killed." The Dutchers said it took about six weeks for the pack to return to normal. The love the wolves share has definitely transferred to our dogs.

Joanne Strinka shares her experience of love with the canine species in the account of Nikki.

NIKKI'S STORY

Nikki came to me as a gift. Not a birthday or Christmas gift, but a true gift. She was gift from Spirit, a gift from Creator, a gift from God.

In spring of 1992, I walked through the front door to my home after a really rough day at work. What I saw was a little fur ball on my couch that looked A LOT like a little black bear cub. After the initial shock had worn off, I asked my roommate, "What and whose is that?". She responded, "It's yours"! I said, "No way do I need another dog", as I already had two. She said, "Well, I am not taking her back, so if you want to get rid of her then that's up to you."

My roommate had gone to the local SPCA, and they had just rescued 150 animals from a shelter in Alabama. When they arrived, no one was taking care of the animals. They were starved. The water was frozen and the animals were frozen to the floor. Most animals had to be cut off the floor. So Nikki had no hair on one side, and I could tell she was very sick. I took her to the vet and found out she was maybe only 5 weeks old. She had frostbite and pneumonia, and my vet said that he thought she was too young and sick to survive. He told me to leave her there and he would do everything he could to try and save her. She stayed there for four weeks. He took her home with him every night. I visited on my lunch hours and after work to see her. Slowly she regained strength. The older she got, the more she looked like a little black bear. Finally, I asked my vet what breed he thought she was. He grinned and said, "You don't know?". I replied, "No, she looks like a bear to me". He grinned again and said, "She's a wolf". Then he said, "She has dog in her too, so that makes her a wolf-dog". I was shocked! I had really never heard of wolf-dogs.

I went to the public library to research wolf-dogs. I couldn't find much information, but what I did find was that they were not good pets. They would eat your house, you could never train them, and there was always the risk of them turning on you.

So now I was really concerned! I found myself constantly thinking of her the four weeks he had her. I felt like I had known her all my life! And the bond I felt with this little sick baby was like nothing I had ever experienced. The day she was finally strong enough to come home was amazing! The night before I went to pick her up, I couldn't sleep. I felt like a little kid that knows she is going to Disney World the next day. I was a wreck at work all day, and the day seemed five days long. When I finally got off work, I jumped in my car and raced to the vet's office! When he handed her to me, it was like nothing I had ever experienced in my life! When her fur touched my hands, I felt a shock. Not a bad shock, just like an electrical vibration. I took her home and let her sleep in my bed. I took her to work with me. This continued for the next 13 years.

As she grew, she acted less and less like a "dog". And the part about them eating your house, all true! I went through three complete sets of furniture in two-and-a-half years – all of it, living room, dining room, bedroom. She even ate a hole through my hardwood floors! Then overnight, she was a different animal. It's like she understood all I had been trying to teach her for those two-and-a-half years in one night.

Over the next few years, she grew into a beautiful, black, long-haired wolf-dog. She appeared to be 100 pounds, but she was only 65. The rest was hair. She had the most amazing ability to know exactly what I was thinking, and I felt like I knew what she was thinking. Years later, I realized our thought vibrations were so close in line that we could understand each other.

Nikki and I did EVERYTHING together. We slept together, we went to work together, we went fishing 100 miles off shore in the Gulf of Mexico together, and we camped on islands together. But Nikki's favorite activity was to ride the wave runner with me! She had her own ski vest. She had her own water shoes – four of them. She would sit in front of me with her front paws on the handlebars. When we would crash and burn, she would be the first one back on the wave runner – tail wagging, looking as if she was grinning from ear to ear. All I could hear was, "Come on Mom! Hurry up! Let's do that again!"

When Nikki was 10, I decided I wanted to get another wolf-dog – partly because I was so worried about losing her and partly because I knew she would help me train him. This turned out to be the turning point in my life.

A neighbor, whom I had told of my idea to get another wolf-dog, came to my house one night to tell me that a guy she worked with had wolf-dog puppies for sale. So that weekend off we went to look at the pups. He lived about an hour-and-a-half away in a rural part of central Florida.

All the way there, I kept telling my neighbor that there is something bigger to this. I feel it. She agreed and said she felt it too. When we arrived at his house we saw every kind of dog, cow, horse, chicken, cat, and pig you could imagine. Animals everywhere! They walked us up to the cage the parents were in to meet them. They were amazing! This was the first time I had ever met a "wolf". Annie was the mom. She was a timber color. She was shedding her coat and needed a bath. She was very shy. Night Moon was the Dad. He was solid white and very dirty. We knelt down to meet them, and we were warned to be careful. He was a "man-eater"! As soon as they uttered those words, he came over and kissed my hands, stuck his nose through the fence, and kissed my face. They took us over to meet the babies. They were in the cage next to the parents. There were five. Four were solid black with white toes and white stars on their chests. One was timber color like its mom. Thinking I was a "wolf-dog expert", I played with one after another and finally picked one out. After paying them for my pup, we headed home.

The whole way I had this nagging feeling. Kind of like that pit of the stomach "you know something is going to happen" feeling. We got home and introduced the baby to Nikki. Nikki looked at me with a look that says, OH HELL NO! Okay, now I was in trouble! Nikki wanted nothing to do with this little baby. She would learn to love her is what I was thinking at this point. Nikki walked around with a serious attitude and looked at me like I had lost my mind!

After a couple of days, Nikki was tolerating the baby. So I knew it was going to be okay, so I decided to give the baby a name. I researched Indian names and came up with Saia, which means little wind. The name fit perfectly! Nikki went out of her way to avoid her at all costs. So after one month, I felt that in the best interest of the baby I should send Saia to live with a friend. She had some land for her to run and romp. Nikki was a very happy girl after that!

About four months later, the same neighbor who went with me to get Saia called and said, "You've got to check out this website! Saia's mom and dad are in a rescue!" So, I looked to find it was true. They were in a rescue in north Florida called Lost Wolf Rescue. I called them and inquired about Annie and Night Moon. They told me that when they came in they were both emaciated. Annie was 37 pounds and was beaten with a shovel. She suffered brain damage from the beating. So *that weekend I went to see them, they were in horrible shape! Tears ran down my face, and I felt a rage inside me like I had never felt before! How could someone do this to such amazing creatures? I had visited them every weekend. Annie was so afraid of people that she would throw herself against the fence to try to get away from you if she even saw you across the five acres from her. Night Moon came around fairly quickly and started trusting two-leggeds again. After five months of working with Annie every weekend, my neighbor and I would lie in the dirt and sit with Night Moon in our laps. We hand-fed him and threw meat to Annie. The whole time I could see in her eyes she wanted to trust again. Annie touched a place in me that only Nikki had before. She touched my soul.*

When I was with Nikki or Annie, my soul was calm. No stress, no problems, no thoughts running through my head. It was just calm. I realized they both taught me a lot more than I had ever taught them. Annie finally came around in that timeframe as well.

During those five months, the president of the rescue stepped down, and I became the new president of Lost Wolf Rescue. I would rescue wolf-dogs from people or animal control agencies. I thought Nikki might like a friend, so I would bring home the ones I thought she would get along with. She wanted nothing to do with any of them. I went to St. Lucie County Animal Control to pick up a rescue wolf-dog from them. I brought him home for the night with every intention of taking him to the rescue in the morning. As soon as Nikki saw him, she claimed him as her own. He was about five months old and emaciated. He didn't have any manners and was just wild. I named him Jake. Someone chained him to a tree and moved. They said he had been there for about a month. No food or water.

She immediately let him know who was alpha! Over the next year and a half, she taught him to be a very good wolf-dog. He was scared to death of getting into a car. One night I wanted to take them both for ice cream. Nikki hopped up into the van and climbed into the seat. She loved going for ice cream! Jake was not going to get in the van no matter what I did. I looked at Nikki and said, "A little help here". She looked at me, did a very big sigh, and jumped out of the van, walked over to him nose-to-nose and just started howling and barking in his face. She then got back in the van, and he followed right behind her. Ever since that day, he jumps right into any vehicle. He could ride from Florida to New York without your ever knowing he is there. Whenever Jake did something wrong, I couldn't even open my mouth before Nikki would be on him telling him all about it! She did all the training of him.

Nikki coughed as I woke one morning. A few hours later, she coughed again. I called my vet and made an appointment for the following day. At the vet's, everything was normal – temperature, lung sounds, blood work, everything. I insisted that something was wrong. He said, "Joanne, she is healthier than most 6-year-olds I see". I kept insisting. So we did X-rays. That is when the world stood still for me. She had nine malignant tumors. I was devastated! That was a Friday. Sunday she was gone.

I felt like my whole world ended. I felt lost. She knew I would fall apart, so she never let me know there was anything wrong to the end. I called a friend to come over. The next thing I knew I had 11 people at my house. It was midnight. They were all still there, not for me, but for Nikki. Three of these people were animal communicators. Before we buried her, Nikki kept telling my friend April, "I taught him well. He'll be a good boy. I taught him well. He'll be a good boy." She yelled at my friend Sandy, "Mommy needs to bring her home now! She needs to save her!" I later found out that Nikki was referring to Saia. She told my friend Dee she wanted to be buried under the oak tree. This was her favorite spot. So we buried her there. We buried her with spirit bird feathers, tobacco, and sage in the Native American tradition to help the spirit move forward. After we were done, we all stood around and talked. We all came to one realization. Nikki had taught every single one of us a huge life lesson! Each person learned a different lesson, but they were all very important ones. For me, Nikki taught that these wonderful creatures are more intelligent than we can understand and that they have much to teach us. She taught me how to listen to the creatures to hear what they have to say. Ever since that night, my front gate, which has been there since before Nikki arrived as a baby, will not stay closed. Nikki and I now have wars over the gate. I close it, she opens it. It's only one side that opens. This sometimes goes on for hours. It's her way of letting me know she is still with me and watching over Jake and me.

Jake   Niki

Joanne Strinka, St. Petersburg, Florida
Lost Wolf Rescue Inc.

The story of Nikki is an amazing one and shows us the love and deep connection that these animals have with us. Our canine friends are deep spiritual beings that will help us grow. They guide us, protect us, and help us. They give us their all, and we should be willing to go that distance for them with their needs. If we can open our hearts, we can receive the message of their love to us and fulfill our lives. Rocky and Sherri have that bond that has allowed Sherri to find her path.

Life with Rocky

It was more than 10 years after the death of my last dog before I was ready for another one. After his death, I moved around a lot, spent years traveling, and time living overseas, all of which are not conducive to having a dog in your life. When I finally decided I was ready for another dog, I discussed it with my husband, who had never before owned a dog or a cat for that matter, something I found hard to imagine. I wanted to make the experience a pleasant one for him, so I researched breeds to find just the right one that I felt would be a good choice for a "first time" dog. I found it - it was a golden retriever, the quintessential family dog.

Long before we had even decided on a breed, our dog had a name – Rocky – after Rocky Balboa of the movie fame. You have to understand, my husband is Italian, born there, raised in New York City, and he wanted our new dog's name to be Italian. So Rocky it was. We researched and found a great breeder outside of Tampa, Florida, and after several months, brought our new bundle of joy home. He immediately worked his way into our hearts and became a beloved member of our family.

Our life with Rocky since then has been such a joy; with lots of love, smiling, laughter, fun hikes, playing at the beach, long walks, romping in the backyard, etc. He has such a love of life and of people, especially children that he will just sit down and watch what's going on, waiting for the opportunity to go greet whoever wants to say hello. It's people he cares about, not other dogs. He has the perfect personality of a service dog and has shown his helpful nature to my husband and others. It was because of his unique personality that I decided to pursue training with him as a therapy dog. When Rocky was about 2 years old, we completed this training together, and now he lifts the spirits of all those that we visit. It's very gratifying to witness the emotional healing that occurs as he sits there and lets people pet him.

I can't recall the number of times I would come home from work, upset, down, and generally disgusted, only to be greeted with such love and happiness that my foul mood disappeared. It's the delight he feels when he sees you that gives you the greatest happiness. His ability to change your mood goes beyond what I have experienced with dogs in the past. He is a caretaker of feelings, I think because he is so in tune with them, both his and ours as humans.

After many years, I noticed that Rocky was starting to exhibit some signs of arthritis, general soreness, inactivity, and general aging symptoms, something to be expected of a dog his age. He still had the personality, loving us, loving life, loving everyone, and I wanted to figure out a way to help cure or relieve any issues he may have. I wanted him to be as healthy and comfortable as possible for as long as possible. That's when I had the dream.

I've been in private industry for many years, and over the last five years, my company has been downsizing. In the past I was stressed about this, so I spent time in earnest looking at other career possibilities in case I decided I no longer wanted to do software design. I even started a part-time business with a friend and after a year or so doing it I decided I really didn't like the business, so I got out.

One night, I had an incredibly vivid dream about what I should be doing as my life's work. It was so vivid that I awoke the next morning and announced to my husband that I was going to do "canine massage". I knew nothing about the mechanics of it at the time and fortunately for me he didn't laugh or tell me I was crazy. He simply said, "Go for it." And so I did. Over the next couple of months, I researched canine massage schools, and found a good one to attend. I enrolled and became certified in September 2006.

Sometime shortly after that, I had another dream, this time, what the name of my business should be. The dream told me "Rocky's Retreat" in honor of Rocky, the special soul who started me on this path. This is where and how my new business began. Since then, my practice has evolved to include Acupressure, Aromatherapeutic Healing and Reiki. I've studied and continue to study Traditional Chinese Medicine, canine nutrition and other means of keeping your dog healthy, both emotionally and physically. I also give workshops on canine massage to people who want to positively affect the lives of their own dogs. I'm the volunteer wellness practitioner with Greyhound Ranch Adoptions, a wonderful local greyhound rescue organization that finds permanent homes for retired racing greyhounds. I work on these dogs on a weekly basis to prepare them for their final loving adoptive homes.

I also work on Rocky on a regular basis. He gets regular massage, acupressure and Reiki, careful diet monitoring, and all the love we can give him. After all, he is the one responsible for me going down this path. He pointed me in this direction.

I truly believe that he knew how to guide me and let me see that my feelings are so important. It is so important to be happy and enjoy life, and to be grateful today and every day. If I do this, then life will bring me everything I could possibly want. That's something I didn't really realize before, but now I know it and live it daily.

This new path has so changed my life for the better; it is filled with joy and purpose, positive people, new experiences, and the knowing that I can help so many people and their dogs have a better quality of life. The reward is beyond description. Having Rocky in my life has truly blessed me.

Sherri Cappabianca, Winter Park, Florida
www.rockysretreat.com

The above story is from a very close friend of mine. Sherri and her husband Pat have been kind to me. They have also cooked some great meals that I have had the pleasure to share. Together, with Rocky lying by our feet, we have enjoyed good wine, good conversation, and great company. I was visiting my good neighbor Jimmy for his birthday celebration late in September when Sherri called to tell me that Rocky had died.

They just recently returned from some traveling, and he was not doing too well. His hips seemed to be bothering him, and he had lost interest in food. They took him to the vet that day to have him checked, and it was not good news. They immediately went on to the specialists for ultrasound, and it was confirmed that he had cancer on his spleen that had metastasized. The vets told them he would only live for two more days. They took Rocky home for some very special time together and later had the vet come to the house to help Rocky pass peacefully. Sherri told me Rocky was gone while in the background my friends were singing *Happy Birthday.* How ironic to be celebrating on one level and saying goodbye on another.

Death always leaves us with that empty feeling and the pain of loss. One minute they are there and the next, *gone*. The time seems to have flown past once they are gone. Of course, there is no suffering any longer by the person or animal who has died, only by those still behind. The feelings are all about our missing the one who is gone. It is healthy to grieve and to feel that loss. Remember to take that time but also remember to celebrate their life. The energy of their spirit has really not died. It has just changed. It has moved into a different form. Energy can never die; it is neither created nor destroyed. Hold that feeling to gain some comfort that our loved ones are still with us, deep in our hearts. The more it hurts, the closer to our hearts they were.

Rocky, you were an amazing dog and I dedicate this chapter to you. You touched my heart, you were a kind soul and you gave people joy. I hope that I can do the same. We will miss you.

On a happy note, Sherri has now brought a new addition to her family – Yankee. A beautiful blood relative of Rocky to share her life. Sherri understands the importance of canine language and is giving Yankee all the proper guidance for a healthy canine mind.

CHAPTER
– *Eight* –

Choose the Right Baggage to
Match Theirs

CHAPTER
-Eight-

Any time a new dog joins your family, whether it is a puppy or a rescue, it is important to understand his process. The first two days the dog will be sniffing out his new surroundings. He needs to get a feel for this new situation. In that timeframe, he may tend to be a little more jumpy or leery of coming to you. Remember, that's fine. Do not add pressure by making eye contact and calling him with all kinds of coaxing. Just give him space. For the next two weeks, the dog will be figuring out where he belongs in this new environment. This is the best time to convey to the dog that you are the leader, that he has nothing to worry about, and that there is no pressure for anything.

With a rescue dog, he may or may not have issues that have come home with him. Some rescue dogs are completely ready to jump right into a new family. This does not mean that they are not going to check out the pack structure in their new home. That is simply a given with every dog regardless of breed. If you came home with a rescue dog that does have issues, then take note: if you are in a mental prison, you will not be able to fully reach your potential, and that is the same with a dog. It is just as important, if not more so, to heed my earlier advice on when he first arrives home. Keep the pressure off and give him space.

JAN MEETS BARMIE, AND BARMIE MEETS JAN

It was a bitter February morning when I found myself walking around the huge animal shelter near my home. I was not looking to expand my family at that time, for I had recently lost my beloved Springer spaniel, Khan, and I was really struggling with not having him with me anymore. One of his lifetime companions, a super Beagle named Kim, was still going strong, with a lively year-old black German Shepherd, Sasha, joining the family. It was also at this time that I had been drawn into the fascinating world of canine behavior, and I was certain I was close to answering why dogs have so many problems in our modern society.

I was desperately unhappy with conventional dog training. It relies on varying degrees of force, and I just had to find another way to work with "man's best friend". Fortunately, I was introduced to the amazing work of Monty Roberts, The Man who Listens to Horses, *in 1989; and, after getting over my initial skepticism, I realized that his technique was based on getting the animal to want to work for you, not because it is made to. I also loved what he had to say about a good teacher facilitating learning and rewarding achievement. Monty had watched* the wild mustangs in Nevada and had seen how they communicate. He then found a way to translate this, so he could imitate the lead animal. I set about learning just how canines communicate by studying wolves, African wild dogs, coyote, and dingoes. To my utter delight, just as Monty has found, they all have a language and rules that we need to understand and mimic to make all undesirable behaviors disappear. This is the key to behavior shaping.

As I looked at the array of dogs all needing a new life, my eyes fell on one, a very thin little Jack Russell, shivering in a corner. "What's his story?" I asked a young kennel maid. "Oh, yes, that one! Well, he was found tied to a rock with a piece of baling twine around his neck. He is very aggressive over food, his mouth is damaged, and we believe that he was either kicked or hit in the face. He runs away from us if he can and growls whenever anyone goes near. He really is not very friendly."

I knelt down, not looking directly at him as the tears came to my eyes. Was it any surprise he didn't like people? The young lady continued, "He is for euthanizing because he is so unpredictable". Immediately, I wanted to rush in, scoop him up, and tell him that I was going to love him, care for him, and put the world right for him. After all, I am a dog lover and wanted nothing more than to put right all the bad, but if I had done that he would have been destroyed that very day, as I would have forced him to bite me.

I had to sign a disclaimer to take him on, and, in all fairness to the management, they only let me have him as they knew of my work. Although they believed I would fail, I was perhaps his best chance. So Sasha, Kim, and I coaxed him from the kennel to my car and he jumped in. Just before I set off, I watched as Sasha – in typical Shepherd's fashion – tipped her head to one side as if to say, "What's your story?"

Once I arrived home, I parked on the drive and closed the gates, lifted the tailgate, and invited Sasha and Kim from the car. They happily jumped out. Barmie stayed pinned in the car growling. I unlocked the back door, went through the utility room into the warm kitchen, and closed the door to the rest of the house because I had a feeling that I was in for a long wait. My cupboards were in need of a thorough clean, so I set about this with my coat firmly secure against the cold, and the waiting began…

One of the most beautiful sights throughout the waiting was how a very concerned Sasha repeatedly went outside to the car and looked at Barmie as if to encourage him out and then return to me, her head on one side. After over two hours, I finally sensed a little presence coming into the kitchen. I had to resist the need to look at him and coax him to me, for the result of doing that would only have been his hasty retreat to the car. I left him alone to work out for himself that there was nothing to fear, and he was able to creep into the room and take up residence in the corner under the table. I quietly closed the back door, something I knew Kim appreciated very much.

I found it very hard not to look at him, but I knew that he had to work things out for himself; my main incentive was to show him that this was a good place to be and food was the best approach. I had been told that he was very protective of food and had snapped at a kennel staffer when they tried to take his food away. Sadly, this approach is too often used. People who use it generally believe it to be a good way to show the dog that you are the leader, but in reality it is completely wrong and results in many dogs being needlessly destroyed. The leader is the provider, so I showed Barmie this quality. I invited the other two into the hall so that I could give my information to Barmie without distraction. I then placed a small amount of food evenly among three bowls (small feeds are often the way to build up an emaciated animal).

Barmie was firmly lodged under the table, and at the sight and smell of the food he began to growl. Without looking at him, I ate a slice of toast I had prepared for myself, and then placed the first dish on the floor and walked away. Trembling and growling, he dashed over to the bowl and devoured the contents. I then placed the second dish on the floor, and he repeated his actions (I remember smiling at his ability to growl and eat at the same time). Finally, I placed the last bowl down and left the room. I gave him a couple of minutes and then returned to the kitchen taking no notice of him at all.

The hardest part of working with dogs in a way that they understand and value is ignoring them whenever we reunite after any separation. Barmie's future depended on me getting it right and going at a slow quiet pace. By the end of day two, he was not growling and began coming forward a little, with a thoughtful expression on his face when I prepared the food. He still rushed to each bowl, but that was just fine.

To my joy, his progress was very quick. Within two weeks, he gained weight and moved freely about the house and garden. There was no growling or trembling, the fear in his eyes was replaced with a sparkle, and he even began to play with the other two dogs. I still hadn't touched him; my needs had to wait, but I was working on that, too. After the evening meals, I would sit on the floor reading. Sasha and Kim would cuddle up alongside me and all was well. Barmie started to make his way toward us, getting a fraction closer each time until, after three weeks, he came right up to me wagging his tail.

I spoke quietly with warmth and realized that what had been a terrified and suspicious dog was now content in my presence. Over the next few days, as he sat by me, I extended a finger to rub his cheek a couple of times. I knew that he wanted more and that was what I wanted *him to feel. He soon got to know if I called him, he would get only affection and kindness. He was with me because he wanted to be, and he knew that he was safe with me.*

He progressed at an amazing pace, and just one month after I first saw him, he would jump onto my lap when invited and be happy to cuddle up. It had happened and our friendship grew stronger. He taught me a lot about how a dog thinks and responds, which are lessons I shall always value. I thank you Barmie for being so patient. You may have gone from my arms, but you will never be gone from my heart.

Jan Fennell, Lincolnshire, England
www.janfennellthedoglistener.com

It is human nature to lavish love on a needy soul. The dog, however, is a different species and needs to have the appropriate type of lavishing at the appropriate time. Remember that I spoke about how to give comfort in the earlier story of Navarre. With rescue dogs, we can certainly feel like we want to make it up to them. We want to show them that all people are not so bad. That is fantastic *if* we do it the right way. Mary Lynne Doleys understands the right way and does her best to help the canines she encounters.

GIVE PEACE A CHANCE

Buddy was a dog I first encountered at the animal shelter where I regularly volunteer. He had only been there a couple of days, and before that he'd been fending for himself on the streets. I can only imagine how terrifying it was to be brought into such a place and kept in a cage for 23.5 hours a day. The first thing I saw on his cage was a note warning people that he was very frightened and that it was difficult to get in and out of the kennel. Far from being a deterrent, this made me want to work with him all the more.

I opened the cage and, without making any eye contact, waited for Buddy to come to me. Before long he did, head lowered and tail tucked. I reached underneath his chin to let him acquaint himself with my hand, and then clipped the leash onto his collar.

Once we got outside, he tended to walk several steps ahead of me. He didn't pull on the lead, as so many troubled dogs do, but walked just out of reach. Each time he got out in front, I silently stopped and stood my ground and he immediately returned to my side. If I called him, then he would come to me, but with a very worried look.

While the shelter was being renovated, foster "parents" were needed to house all the dogs, and without hesitation I requested Buddy. When he arrived at my house, I let him check the place out, and he promptly found my dog's bed and made himself at home. Although he got along fine with my Golden Retriever, Pandora, Buddy didn't want to play with her in the first days.

It quickly became apparent that Buddy had been abused in his former life; this explained why he wisely kept out of reach (of human hands) while on lead. There were times when he thought he was "in trouble" with me and would crouch, then roll on his side in submission, awaiting punishment. This I found absolutely heartbreaking. I cannot imagine what kind of person had abused such a wonderful, affectionate creature and then put him out on the street.

I kept a record of the progress Buddy made each day he spent in my home. When he first arrived, he wanted to follow me everywhere and became extremely distressed every time I left the house. But within a few weeks he accepted my departures with only a few barks to let me know his displeasure. I can't take all the credit for Buddy's recovery. Pandora, with her clownish antics, was able to persuade Buddy to play with her in just four day's time. I had never been able to entice him to play at the shelter. After a few weeks in my home, he even began retrieving a ball for me, although I suspect he did it more to make me happy than out of any love for the game.

In the end, a lovely couple adopted Buddy. They prepared their home for his arrival and kept in touch with me about how to resolve behavioral issues and to let me know how he was progressing. They gave him a new name along with a fresh start, and now we meet for occasional play dates for Buddy and Pandora. When I see him now, I see not only a dog who is fit, healthy, and well-loved, but one who no longer fears human strangers or ducks at the sight of a raised hand. This is what this dog has deserved all along. And this special dog really showed me he could understand that not _all_ humans have let him down, so he was willing to learn to trust people again. Buddy was able to let go of his past and overcome some difficult obstacles.

If Buddy could do this, then I knew these were lessons to learn from such a good little canine teacher. Although at the time I never thought of him as the teacher, he showed me a lot that I can take into my own life. I shall always remember those lessons, especially when I feel that I want to give up on people for the things they do to dogs. I can remember that Buddy did not give up; we can always find the good ones.

Mary Lynne Doleys, Chicago, Illinois
www.peacefulpaws.us

Another dog whose past might hinder them is the retired racing Greyhound. These dogs come off the track, and if they are one of the lucky ones, then a rescue can intervene and save their lives. Thousands of Greyhounds are killed every year in the racing industry, but it still continues. It is interesting that the issue of stopping dog fighting is so prominent, but little attention is paid to the plight of racing dogs.

The Greyhound is a dog bred for speed. When they come off the track, they do not know much about what life is like in our world. Most have never been up steps or on carpet. Many will be aggressive to cats or small dogs because they are similar to what these dogs chased on the track. Most of them do not care about much; they just want a sofa and a tranquil life like any other dog. They are a quiet breed that loves to sleep. If you are a cat person, a Greyhound is the dog for you (providing you find a cat-friendly dog). It is a testament to the dog world that these dogs are willing to let go after being in such poor conditions and give us humans another shot. The tireless work of the Greyhound rescuers is ongoing. I personally work with Leslie Woliner of the Greyhound Ranch Adoptions in Florida. Leslie helps transition Greyhounds to forever homes, and we have both seen the value that these dogs give to people's lives. One of my clients has a dog named Gabi and remarks how good she feels when she gets home after a hectic day to spend time with her relaxed couch potato.

Baggage comes in all shapes and sizes. The Greyhound certainly do experience their share as do other rescue dogs. Pooh Bear is not a Greyhound, but in my next story, you will meet a little girl with a lot of baggage.

THE NOODLE

One hot summer afternoon in Florida, I took a ride out to a nearby horse rescue. I chatted with the director at a luncheon and took her up on an offer for a tour. While I met the horses, I noticed several dogs running around. One was an adorable 8-week-old Border Collie puppy. When I was ready to leave, I was asked if I could find the puppy a home. Out on this 40-acre property, a puppy doesn't stand a chance against the eagles and other predators. So I took Pooh Bear home with me. She was very nervous in the car and got carsick. When I got her home, she went through the usual quarantine procedures, and before long she was introduced to the pack. I noticed she was a very shy and timid dog. You might say she had very little self-confidence. Pooh was a sweet girl but really needed to come out of her shell.

Since she was a Border Collie (not to stereotype or anything), I got some Frisbees. She had a natural talent and was very interested in the new game. I was not a very good Frisbee thrower and had no experiences with disc dog work, but we started to learn together. After awhile, Pooh had built up her stamina and went for the long throw. She was super-dog.

As time went on, I noticed Pooh had gained a lot more self-confidence. She now started to display herding behavior with the cats. She would get the low stance with her head down and focused on the uncomprehending felines. The cats didn't know what to do about another house pet trying to make them walk single-file into a closed space, and some just smacked her. To that Pooh barked back. As more time went on, I noticed her self-confidence strengthen. She now began herding the horses! At first, she was quite concerned with their size, but in just a short amount of time she had blossomed.

I learned from Pooh that you just need to give dogs the time and space to get comfortable. Do not rush and overwhelm them. When they start to settle in, they will show you when they are ready. For Pooh, it was the Frisbee that brought her out of her shell. For another dog, it might be a ball or a romp in the park. Others may just need a cushion and a nice pat on the head, at the right time of course. The dogs are willing to open up to new things, places, and people if we let them. Give them time and space, and take these same lessons into your world. Realize different dogs have different personalities and work with that. Foster parents and guardians out there and even parents, if you try one thing to help and it does not work, go to something else. The key is to not let frustration set in and to keep things relaxed. Take it a little at a time and let time work. You can also use this same mentality with yourself in a new situation. Realize that something new will feel uncomfortable. Allow that, flow with it rather than against it. Give it time to feel right and keep your mind in a relaxed state, and then you will find your way.

People have as much baggage as their dogs do. It does not matter where we were in the past. What is important is that we know where we are now and that we take the steps necessary to "grow forward". Dogs help show people the way as much as we can show them the way.

JOANNA'S STORY

The summer when I was 9, we had moved to a small town for my father to install a phone system in a new office. My brother and I spent a lot of time on a farm that was owned by a friend of my father's. That summer my brother constantly abused me. It was years before I was able to put it all together and understand why. He was lashing out at me because of his relationship with our father.

The best way to describe my father was Archie Bunker. My father abused my brother, and then, out of anger and frustration, my brother physically abused me. All of the physical and emotional abuse from my parents and brother made me feel useless, which carried over into adulthood. The only thing that got me through my childhood was my dog. I remember sitting and holding him and crying for hours. Many nights I would go to sleep praying not to wake up.

My parents hated my first husband. That is probably why I married him, it was a way out. In my marriage, if I said or did anything out of line, I suffered terrible abuse. When I finally left him, I found myself back at my parents, because I did not know how to take care of myself and I did not believe in myself. People do not understand why women don't just leave. It is not that easy. When abuse is all you have ever known, it is normal. I can understand how an abused animal just sits and takes it. There is truly that feeling of learned helplessness.

I rebounded from one relationship to another. I spent over two years in counseling. What I have found is that even today when I have a lot on me I go back to my dogs. I have never felt whole without a dog in my life. I spent many hours alone with my dogs and in the mountains. What the dogs have always shown me was that my past did not matter. The simple acts of loving them and caring for them was all it took. The dogs were always happy to live in the moment, to enjoy the sun, and to not worry about tomorrow but to chase that butterfly today.

Joanna Furuglyas, Lakeland, Florida
www.gotojoanna.com

Joanna has come from a place that is very difficult for many people to let go of. The same can be said for many dogs in rescue centers as well. Some abusive situations will have had an effect that will take time and patience and the proper guidance for the dog to be able to move on. A "remembered pain" may always stay with a dog, but when you give the dog the things it needs for a happy and relaxed life, the prior bad experiences can be left in the past and the dog can lead a completely fulfilled life.

Deanna Deppen from the Shy Wolf Sanctuary has encountered her share of experiences with all types of dogs. She also understands that the baggage can be left at the door.

Yukon's Story

I met Yukon the Monday after our first open house celebrating Shy Wolf Sanctuary's incorporation. We were planning a modest get-together to promote helping the animals when the local newspaper caught wind and featured a photo of Michael Kloman and Cody the wolf-dog. The event grew beyond anything we'd imagined. In the midst of all the last-minute preparations we got a rescue call about a wolf-dog in Ft. Myers.

The lady's son had bought Yukon from a breeder as a puppy. The son now needed testing and medical care. She wanted help placing the dog since she'd had so many calls on him and she didn't want to have to make the drive to continue caring for Yukon. We promised to help right after the weekend. The event came and went, and we called the lady back, only to hear that she'd found a home for the dog.

Two days later, we received a call from another lady wanting to place a dog named Yukon with us. With more inquiries we found out that the original buyer was a deaf mute man who had taken all of his frustrations out on the dog. Yukon had a strong prey drive and a terrible fear of men. The first couple that had taken him kept him only one night before calling the woman and asking for the name of another adopter. The next family kept him two days but had small children and many small animals on their farm, all perfect for Yukon to chase! In desperation this lady had called the zoo to try and find a more appropriate home for this obviously abused and fearful animal. We said to bring him down.

Upon arrival Yukon was a one-year-old that was so terrified of men he wouldn't even let a woman in a baseball cap approach. He was skinny and shaking and really didn't know what to think after having four homes in five days! It took lots of love and patience to bring Yukon around. It was 8 months before he'd even allow a man to approach him. Many more months, and years, went by before he was able to develop trust for men and to form a strong bond with them.

I brought Yukon to my house as a foster since he needed so much TLC. At the time, I had a bossy husky named Rajah that had been rescued years earlier. He was my "trainer" for dealing with hurt, abused, and neglected animals since he had been all three. Rajah befriended Yukon, and the two of them would run and play.

I noticed that Rajah's health was declining and arranged for some testing. The results were devastating when I was told he had cancer and that there was a tumor positioned to penetrate a major blood vessel. If that happened, he would die a slow and painful death, so I was given no option but to help Rajah cross, and sooner rather than later.

It was Friday the 13th when my closest friends gathered to help me send Rajah off. We'd gone to the beach that day and he'd had some ice cream. That was the only thing I could coax him to eat. Christa, Michael, Dana, Nancy, Dr. Baker and her assistant, Yukon, and I all gathered in one room. Rajah went from person to person saying his goodbyes. Some of these people, like Michael, he'd never really warmed up to before that day. When he was done, Rajah came to me and stood, as if to say "I'm ready" and he lay down. The vet administered a sedative and then the final shot as he lay still.

In the room watching all of us, Yukon took this scene in as it unfolded. Just as Rajah took his last breath, Yukon walked up to him and *sniffed his muzzle. He then walked directly to me and kissed me on the face as if to say, "He's good, He's home". Yukon then wandered off and moved on with whatever he had to do next.*

He's since been adopted by a couple, staying by his mistress while she was in the hospital, mourning her loss with her husband, and challenging him to take their relationship to new levels of trust. Prior to Angelita's passing, Tom had minimal interaction with Yukon. After all, he was a lady's dog and held grudges against men that seemed forged in steel. Slowly but surely those dissolved due to Tom's determination to do whatever was necessary to win over Yukon's trust.

Tom had lost both Angelita and his elder dog, JB, in a few short weeks. The gap between man and dog seemed to be growing larger. We tried a companion dog that we knew got on well with Yukon. He adored Nakipa. She, on the other hand, got bored with the quieter life away from the hustle and bustle of the sanctuary. Just when we were wondering if this truly would work out, a rescue friend named Debra offered to place one of her personal dogs with Tom and Yukon.

This particular dog was a happy-go-lucky malamute that had been rescued at 4 months of age. She's never met a stranger and has an outgoing and loving personality. Deb and I both felt she was exactly what Yukon and Tom needed! Plans were made and the three of us (Tom, Yukon, and I) made the 13-hour trek to get Petunia. How could one go wrong with a dog named Petunia?! She wasn't immediately sure she liked Yukon, but she loved Tom, and Deb knew her well enough to know she'd come around in four or five days. Right on schedule, "Cutie Petutie" decided that Yukon wasn't so bad, and now they are inseparable. Yukon even started vying for attention rather than letting her get all the loving. Tom bought four acres of wooded ground and fenced it in. Yukon and Petunia rule the property and are expected every morning at the coffee klatch, having won over even diehard doubters.

Animals are in tune with energy and the circle of life and death. They accept what is natural and have a huge capacity to forgive and to trust again. Though it took time, Yukon has demonstrated that we can all overcome our past and move on to a healthier and happier existence.

Deanna Deppen, Naples, Florida
www.shywolfsanctuary.org

Living with a pack of dogs is a true joy, but it is a big responsibility as well. There are times that pack life is not so easy. Most of my learning about the dogs, about myself, and about life originates from the pack. My current pack is eight rescue dogs. Of course, there are also the adoptables that come into the rescue. My eight pack have all come through the door of In Harmony with Nature, my rescue organization. It is always a special case that touches my heart, and I know right away if they will stay. Even if I want them to stay, if it is in their best interests, then I push my feelings aside and find them a forever home. In the case of canine confrontations, this is sometimes the best thing for the dog. It is vital that all members of your pack are happy and that they are living fulfilled lives.

In a pack structure, we hear a lot about the alpha. On the other side of the coin is the omega. This is the lowest member of the pack, and it is not an easy position to be in. In the wild, the omega has the option of leaving the pack. There are even times when the omega will get forced out of the pack. And there are times when the omega will stay in the pack and endure the position they find themselves in. Once your dog becomes an omega, it is very hard to rebuild their self-esteem and keep them out of that position. It is our job as protector of our pack to not let the life of a low-ranked member be a miserable one.

In our packs, the omega cannot choose to leave. We cannot determine the structure and, within reason, we cannot interfere with that structure. If we always feed the one we feel is higher, or treat them like they are higher, then we set ourselves up (as well as the dogs) for failure. The pack structure can change, and we may not pick up on it. That is why you must always convey you are still a capable leader. Your dog will always ask in a different situation, "Okay, who's in charge now?" or "Okay, are you still in charge now?". They will test each other during the reunite situations to reestablish their places as well. If a place changes and you do not see it, you can very well create a problem and cause a fight. As one dog ages, its position may change, and it is up to us to protect that older dog. Sometimes that protection means separation of your pack.

I love having a pack of dogs, but it is not for everyone. Only let your pack grow as you grow with knowledge of yourself and knowledge of the dog language. Let me share some stories of what the pack has taught me over the years in the area of canine confrontation.

LITTLE LION IN WOLF'S CLOTHES

There I was in the vet's office with a sick cat. The door opened and a guy walked in holding a puppy. The pup was obviously injured, blood dripping from its foot. The man found it next door at the front of a store. After handing me the puppy, the man said to the front desk staff, "I have to go, got to get to work". Then the inside door opened and the technician called our name to come in the back. As I held the puppy, and the tech brought the cat carrier in. The vet told the tech to take the pup to the back kennels. He said there was a box out front this morning but it was empty. The pup must have gotten out and wandered over to the convenience store. Lucky little pup, maybe. The vet looked across the room at the foot and due to the severity of the injury quickly surmised that it required amputation. Then he said they might have to put him down. After all, that type of surgery was expensive, and, being a stray, no one was going to pay the bill. I asked the vet how much it would cost and he said, "Honey, you could help a lot more animals out with what the cost of this one puppy's care is going to be". So the tech took him in the back, and I couldn't get that little puppy out of my head.

Leaving the office in tears, I could not believe this beautiful, adorable little baby was going to be killed just because he had no owner. Actually, I could believe it, but I just really hated it. I dropped the cat off at home and went to another appointment. While on my way home, I realized I had forgotten to get the prescription cat food at the vet's.

Once I returned to the office, I saw the tech who had taken the puppy. I asked her if they had put him down. She said they had gotten so busy that there was no time. He was still in the back, and she asked if I wanted to see him. I rushed down that hall to get to the little one. They took me to his cage, and he just sat there with the cutest little purple tongue sticking out and a horrible-looking injury to his rear leg. His entire little foot, the whole hock, had been de-gloved! I opened the door and he licked my hand. With that, his fate was sealed. I didn't care how much it cost; I was going to save this one. I learned my lesson with Phoenix, and this boy had crossed my path so it was meant to happen.

As with all things in life, everything happens for a purpose, and I totally forgot to get the cat food that day because my vibrations were putting out that I wanted to help that puppy. So the Law of Attraction went to work and kept the facility busy, so I could get back there to save this life. The tech took me back into a room, and Dr. Hall appeared. He said this was not going to be easy, but he would help. He looked at the pup's foot and had the idea to use a wet/dry bandage treatment to see if we could save the foot. The first step was to sedate him, thoroughly clean the foot, and give it a good look over.

Later that day, I went back again with Ellen, and we saw the pup. He had a huge bandage on the leg and was a little groggy but doing fine. His treatment required him to stay hospitalized for a week, but I was able to visit anytime I wanted. While he was there, we named him Simba. He looked like a little lion cub.

All four of the vets at Powers Drive Animal Hospital helped with his care. Over the course of the week, I assisted the vets with bandage changes, so I would know how to continue once we got home. Dr. Bacia, Dr. Sardenga, and Dr. Yerger all got to know me well. By the end of the week, the dog was ready to go home. Simba required almost daily bandage changes, but we saved his leg.

Now began the drama. This little boy acted like you were killing him when we worked on him. We were in no way causing him any pain, but he would scream. I jumped and dropped the bandage, so we switched roles and Ellen changed while I held him. After awhile, I realized he was much calmer when only one person did the work. His little foot was healing, but he never let it slow him down; and when he was introduced to the pack, he was quickly accepted.

Navarre was a wonderful big brother. One thing that I was going to have to watch for was how the other dogs treated Simba, given that he was an injured dog. In a pack of dogs, being injured can mean trouble. In the wild, Simba would not survive, and an injured dog can be very dangerous. As time progressed, it become apparent Simba had issues. Even though he received the right leadership from me, he still displayed an injured dog behavior within the pack. He was very protective of his personal space with the other dogs, as well as the cats. He became aggressive and very vocal if he felt threatened. If there was any rise in excitement level, like someone coming to the house (a perceived danger situation), he had an aggressive outburst to chase everyone away from him.

When you know what is going on, you can deal with it. If you did not understand the situation you would say he was a hair-trigger aggressive dog. I knew better and understood how to control the situation. Simba was never left alone in the pack and always supervised for his, as well as the pack's, protection. Simba is a very playful boy, but a tough dog. He is so vocal even when he plays that most people think he is being aggressive. Most other dogs think that, too, and are afraid to engage him in play. He needs a very self-confident, tough dog that doesn't take offense at the way he plays. I don't know many owners who could handle him the right way. And he has only had one other dog that has been a great play partner for him. It is definitely a plus that I have been with him to know exactly what he went through and how he is. He is not adoptable, but that is fine. I would never want this boy to go anywhere.

Simba has really helped me to see just how important it is to understand someone before you simply pass judgment on them. You may never know what has happened to them, and they may act a certain way toward you that is confusing. Their reaction to you could be circumstantial, and if you can control your feelings, then you may get some great results. This is a reminder that you are the one responsible for your life and feelings, and for the results that you get.

BROTHERS FIVE

Earlier, I talked about the Brothers Five and the puppy fights. Well, as time went on, the three brothers that are still part of my pack continued to interact very well together. They have established their hierarchy and it occasionally changes, but for the most part everyone is a cohesive unit.

In the pack, feeding time can be a cause for confrontation. My dogs are fed a raw diet the way nature intended, and they are very happy and healthy dogs. Meal time is not only for sustenance, but also for enrichment. I am not here to tell you how to feed your dogs, and if you feed your dogs dry food, then the situation is the same. In a pack after a kill, hierarchy plays a big role in the order in which you eat. The alpha male and female eat first and most often. As they move off the kill, it is their signal that they have finished and the next in line can eat. On a large kill, several higher ups may all be eating at the same time, but if they move too close to an alpha, then they will be told off. The only wolves attempting to take the food away are the subordinate members who want to see if they can or will be allowed. When people stick their hands in the bowl, they very well deserve to be told off. You are acting like a subordinate, not a leader.

The temperament tests to show food aggression by sticking a fake hand in a bowl of food are just plain wrong. You may agree to disagree with me on that, but I did not make the rules, the wolves did. It is a serious break in communication between humans and dogs, and many dogs are killed because of that test. I understand safety for children with dogs and food bowls, but children should never be left unsupervised around a dog, and a dog should never have food left in their bowl after they walk away from it. All food should be immediately picked up. Not only does this keep the issue with children out of the equation, but it also shows the dog you control the food. They leave it; they lose it. In the Amichien Bonding method, there is a lot more to working with food and many of the behaviors I have discussed.

When I feed my group, we are outside, so there is enough space for everyone. Anyone who might cause an issue is fed separately. If one dog finishes quickly and gets too close to another dog, then there may be a brief confrontation, but most of the time a slight lip curl is all it takes. It usually does not require any action except to be a calm, confident presence there to make sure it does not escalate. Fights over food can get intense if the intention of the other dog *is* to take the food. Keeping the other dogs out of the fight helps the situation, and keeping your cool is paramount to stopping it.

Never stick your hands in the fight. It will serve you better to use a water hose, broom stick (not to beat them with but to push in between them), or, if inside, a heavy blanket. If you have suspect dogs, it is good to keep a harness on them, and you might even need to trail a lead so you can grab something. Use caution when pulling one dog, as to not cause greater damage to the other. After the fight, separate the two into isolated areas and allow the situation to settle. Do not interact with either of the dogs for a good bit of time, but do not feel anger because this is just part of pack mentality. As the leader, simply deal with the situation in a calm, confident, convincing manner. Have the right attitude.

Thumbs Up

Play is another time that can often create canine confrontation. In a pack, if certain dogs are close in rank and the play is getting rough, it could spur a fight. One night I arrived home around nine p.m. after an evening appointment and decided to quickly let all the dogs out together for a last potty before bed. At that time, I had one dog that needed to be closely monitored with my pack or a fight could start. This was a Pit Bull named Dutchess. She was an adoptable dog that stayed in my house with my pack but remained separated most of the time. Dutchess was good with most of the dogs, but if there was any excitement, then she would go into attack mode on one of two dogs that were slightly less self-confident.

Lucy, a Lab mix, was also an adoptable dog that was staying with my pack. She got along pretty well with everyone unless toys were involved. I had no intention of letting anyone start to play because this was "quick go potty" and then in for the night. While all the dogs were out in the garden, I decided to step outside that fence into the horse paddock to feed hay for the evening. In just a couple of minutes, I could walk to the hay shed, throw out a few flakes of hay, and walk back into the garden. My sight of the dogs was never obstructed.

So, as I was returning to the garden, Lucy began to play with Dutchess. This was fine with me because the two played well together – until that night. Lucy had just started a heat cycle and, feeling all high and mighty, started to play quite intensely. As I stepped into the garden, the play turned into a fight. Lucy grabbed Dutchess by the side of the head and began attacking her. In less than a minute from when I walked back into the garden, the fight brought immediate attention from the other members of the pack, and in a split second, another fight broke out between two males. I thought that since it had just started I could easily pull Lucy off Dutchess. I reached in to grab Lucy by her lower body, but somehow at that very moment the dogs turned.

Dutchess retaliated against Lucy, who was seriously attacking the Pit Bull's head. Well, Dutchess inadvertently bit my hand, and in an instant I felt a fire sear through my thumb. This was a pain I had never felt in my entire life. I saw something come out of my thumb and the only feeling was fire. Now, I had nine dogs, one of which was a 12 week old puppy, two fights, and one hand to deal with it all. With my good hand, I pushed off the other dogs from joining in. I went to the bedroom door and opened it and called the dogs. Five of the dogs came in, and I went back to the males and was able to push them apart. They wanted to start in again at each other, but in a stern voice told them to back off and brought them both in. I put one in the bathroom to make sure their tempers would cool.

Back again to the original fight now. Lucy finally let go, and Dutchess ran off. I took Lucy by the collar and then had to try to open the door. I had only one hand, so I put her between my legs and got the door opened. I crated Lucy and then went to look for Dutchess. She was too scared to come out, and I needed to deal with my hand. I went back inside and down the hall to another bathroom. I rinsed the blood off and saw something thin stuck to my hand. I called Ellen to let her know there had been a fight. When she arrived at the house, I said I needed to go to the hospital. I asked her to get Dutchess first and I quickly looked her over. She had some deep punctures but nothing life-threatening, so we knew we could leave her. We crated her and it was off to the hospital for me.

I could not feel anything in my thumb and the pain went all the way up to my elbow. I felt horrible, and now I also needed to report a dog bite. Luckily, all the dogs were up to date on their rabies shots, so I wasn't concerned about that; I could easily deal with the required 10 day in-home quarantine. When I got to the hospital, it was another 30-minute wait, and I was sure it was because I was so calm and composed. I have a high pain tolerance, and I did not come in screaming and writhing. I should have known better because I *was* in a lot of pain.

The things to follow would make you cringe, but basically while attempting to clean the wound, they discovered that the "stringy thing" hanging out of my thumb was my nerve. The way they discovered that was when the tech started to clean it and moved it; it sent me hollering and had me jump up in immediate excruciating pain. The tech then states, "Oh, wait a minute, that's not a piece of skin, it's your nerve". Thank you very much!

To "snip" a long story short, they "cut" my nerve off and sent me home. They said go see an orthopedic doctor within two days. *Nice.* Well, it has been over a year since that happened, and I still have no feeling even after a special procedure to attempt to get the nerve to grow back together. I am left-handed, and this was my left thumb. I did have to learn to do things differently, and to this day it does not feel like my thumb on my hand, it feels like something foreign. I no longer let it bother me and do my best to mentally work on the re-growth and healing, and over the last four months, I have noticed some strange changes in the way it feels.

The moral of the story, besides not sticking your fingers – or thumb – where they don't belong, is that things can change in an instant within the pack. You must be prepared. One thing I learned in the fire department was complacency kills. You must remember that this is a pack of little wolves. If you are doing things right, you are the leader and are aware. Watch, but have a good time, too. It really is a joy to watch the pack play and interact and groom each other and enjoy life.

Your pack will be in tune with your vibrations. This is a major concern if your life is in upheaval or disarray. If you have a pack, then this is a formula for disaster. If you have one or two dogs you might get away with it, but you would still greatly benefit from listening. And if you have a highly sensitive dog, you should really listen. When I look back to the times when the Brothers Five were puppies and having fights, and then look at my life just prior to the incident with my thumb, I know I brought about those situations. What do I mean by that? Well, during both of those timeframes, my life was not calm, I was not confident in who I was, and I most certainly could not convince anyone I was a leader. My *attitude* was not right. I was not right with me. The Brothers Five timeframe had me dealing with physical issues that were causing me mental issues as well. I was depressed, I had anxiety attacks from PTSD issues, and I had a hard time giving a pack of dogs what they needed.

Tucson, Fawkes, & Bennu

The more recent issue was during a time when my life grew too chaotic. I was disorganized and felt overwhelmed. I was experiencing financial difficulty, too. If we realize just how important our vibrations are to those around us and those affected by us, we might be a bit more careful. Our dogs are a great barometer for our feelings. Yes, there are times when it is just something the dog is doing, but if you are not making progress, *and* you are doing things the proper way to communicate with your dog, then there is a problem. Look deep inside and be honest with yourself. Take a deep breath and relax and identify the issue. Once you have identified the problem, you can find the solution.

Whatever it takes, make the start by making the decision. It is what any good leader would do. *Decide* to have the right attitude. Decide to be calm, outside *and* in. Decide to have confidence in yourself and your pack (the whole pack, people included), and decide to be convincing. The first person to convince is you, and since you have made these decisions, you have already started. Change your life by starting with your vibrations.

CHAPTER
– Nine –

Happy and in Control

CHAPTER
–*Nine* –

As the director of an animal rescue organization, I have the opportunity to see a great deal of the problems that involve our canine companions. Many people start off on the wrong foot with a dog before they even choose one. Most people are unaware of the simple little things that can give you a better chance of selecting the right dog for their personality. Once they have the dog, people often unintentionally run into behavior problems, and that is why so many dogs end up in shelters, with organizations like mine, or worse euthanized. Many of these problems can be easily solved with a little people educating. Children create another area that can bring great pleasure to your canine experience, or great concern. We are going to begin this chapter with some helpful guides to know prior to getting the dog.

Let's start with some information for when you are ready to go get that new family member. Taking the time now will ensure you remain happy and in control with your new pack member.

LET'S CHOOSE A NEW PUPPY, SHALL WE?

Choosing a puppy can be a great time. It is a day of joy when you get to see the litter all together, and it can often be difficult picking just one. If you have gone to a breeder, they should (but may not always) be able to guide you based on your personality to which dogs would be the best fit for you. So you can go in fully armed and aware, I will give you some pointers. As you read this, think about when you see a garden full of children and you will see a lot of similarities.

The breeder knows how the puppies suckle and can say which one would get to the teat first. These are your dominant characters, while the ones who had to struggle or were pushed to the back are going to be your shy pack members. Ask the breeder this specific question so you can make an informed decision. Watch as the puppies play, those same dominant pups will take the toy away from a litter mate, and you will also notice the ones that sit off watching the situation. These are the ones who will be your thinkers. They will weigh a decision in life rather than just barrel forward.

In the litter, you will see several different personality types. As you watch them interact naturally, see if you can distinguish which is which. Then, as you take each one and hold it so it is supported and feels cradled, turn the pup on its back while it is in your arms. Now you are holding it like an infant. This is only done for a short time, about 10 seconds. From this test as Jan Fennell describes in her book *The Seven Ages of Man's Best Friend,* you can discover the personality of your new puppy. These personalities include:

- The Defiant One. Some puppies simply will not stand for it. The moment you turn them over they will immediately right themselves. They will repeat this process every time you try. This dog is going to grow into a strong character, an alpha type. It will take strong, firm, and clear leadership to keep it on the straight and narrow.

- The Resistance Fighter. This one will fight you at first, but will eventually comply and lie on its back, under protest. This again is a dog that may present a few problems, but one who will respond to the right signals.

- The Thinker. Some puppies will initially lie down willingly. They will stay there for a couple of seconds then spring back upright. This indicates a dog that has weighed the situation, come to a decision – that it doesn't like this – and acted upon it. This is a dog that has a lot of courage and intelligence.

- The Cool Customer. Some pups will present no resistance whatsoever; they will simply go limp and lie there. This is a chilled out, laidback individual. With the right guidance, this is going to be a relatively trouble-free dog.

- The Bundle of Nerves. Some puppies will curl up in a ball almost fatally. This is a sure sign of nervousness in the dog. A dog that reacts this way is going to be prone to anxiety attacks when it hears loud noises or is faced with strange situations. In the worst case, it may develop problems, like wetting itself. By identifying them as nervous dogs, however, you can factor this personality into your life with the dog and act accordingly, and hopefully avoid problems.

When you look for the right pup to start a new life with you, there are some other important things to remember. The choice of breed should reflect your lifestyle. If you enjoy grooming, then get a long-haired dog. But if you live in a hot climate, a short coat may be better. If you are giving the dog the right signals, then you can have a calm Jack Russell, and if you are giving the wrong signals, then you can have a hyper Labrador. Do not stereotype the breed. It is true that herding dogs are more geared to working, especially herding, and that hounds tend to be good hunters. Where people go wrong is saying that all Chihuahuas are snappy and all Labradors are laidback. It is the equivalent of saying all Frenchmen wear berets or all Englishmen are football hooligans.

Another important point to consider is this: everyone is excited on the day you pick up your puppy, especially because puppies are so cute. When you arrive, keep yourself and the rest of your human pack calm. Your excitement and energy will cause more excitement and energy in the whole situation. Remember the Law of Attraction. What you put out is what you get. Take a deep breath before you open the car door and relax. You are the new leader going to find a new pack member and *you* want to give a first good impression as well. I am not saying that you must be this stoic figure with no emotion. Guard your emotions for five minutes and pay no mind to the pups. Then welcome them to you and enjoy the cute little creatures that they are. Again, I would still keep myself from getting into all that high-pitched squealing that often goes on around the little ones. This is especially important if the human children are with you.

Ask them to show some restraint as well. This is a great lesson for when they get home and begin to interact with the new addition. This is a very important time, and your awareness should reflect that. As you project the personality of the puppy you want, that is the one that will appeal to you. But if you are projecting a bundle of excitement and are unable to control yourself, asking 500 questions before you even get one answer, that is what you are going to get – a spinning, whirling, jumping bundle of energy that answered your vibration.

Now, if you are going to the rescue center to pick a puppy or a dog, realize that the stress level in an institutional-type setting will alter many dogs' personalities. The dogs have been coming from all the wrong signals and maybe even from all the wrong people. This is like a refugee camp. Basic needs are getting met, but fulfillment is not quite there. This is, of course, no fault of the facility. You can only do so much for these dogs in your care, and the quicker a forever home is found the better for the dog. If the rescue is a private organization, the setting is usually – *usually* but not always – a more relaxed and inviting atmosphere. If you are at the typical shelters, then as you look down the rows of dogs, keep your eyes from making direct contact with the animals. Give side glances to pick out the ones you want to meet.

When you get to the area you can meet the dog, let it come in again without pressure from you, keeping your eyes off him, and let him check out the situation. Give him a minute to calm down. Then in a gentle tone, call the dog or invite him to you and get to know him a little better. When you find the dog and bring it home, again follow the pack rules – no pressure, no eye contact, give it space, but do show it where to do its business, of course. When the dog is settled in, you can give it all the love and affection you want. Just remember to keep it on your terms.

Mindset in starting on this trip to the rescue should also be one of positive vibrations. We do not need to add to the feelings of sadness and despair. Yes, many facilities kill the dogs after just a few short days, and many dogs never find good homes. It does them no good for all of us to put out negative feelings in this situation. Go into these facilities with joy in your heart that you are helping the situation by bringing someone home. I know this is not easy to do, but can you imagine how these poor dogs feel when there is such a gloom hanging over their heads. Come in with lifted spirits and give the dogs that vibration. You may very well be able to help another dog that perks up because of the joy in your heart, instead of causing them to shut down and be passed up by the next visitor.

Another area that is helpful to remaining happy and in control is if your kids learn how to deal with dogs. Kids will meet other dogs at their friends' homes or at the grandparents. After you have brought that new puppy or rescue dog home, the level of activity and noise in the household can be enough to shake even the steadiest surgeon's nerves. Teaching kids the dog language is just as important since they are pack members, too.

Frequently incidents between kids and dogs revolve around food. "Daddy, he took my pizza", or "Mommy, he ate my piece of cake". It is important to instill that when the kids have food they are to sit at the table, not look at or tease the dog, and finish their treat. There should be at least a visual contact between the adults and the dog to make sure the dog is not in the child's personal space and that the child is not feeding the dog.

When kids are around, there almost certainly will be a time when they will be in the presence of a dog with food. Teach the children that they are to stay away if the dog is eating, and the parents should be there to supervise. Remember, the dog should not be having free access to his food in the first place.

Instill in the kids to respect the dogs. It is okay to pet the dogs and to touch the dogs. It is not acceptable to hit them, pull on their fur or to harm them in any way. Gentleness and kindness is the key. Teach the kids to mention the dog's name as they are walking near them, especially if the dogs are sleeping. They should learn that they should not surprise a dog. The kids should not tease the dog, either physically or with food, and should not feed them. Only allow the kids to put the leash on the dog and work with them if they are supervised.

No matter how gentle the dog is, *always* tell and work with the kids to keep their faces away from the dog's face. I do not mean a dog reaching out and licking a face. But rather, do not allow a child to put his or her face in close to a dog's face. The dog may view this as an intimidating signal and react accordingly.

Make a list for the kids and post it on the refrigerator as a reminder of the things to do for the new member. Teach them a few at a time before the dog gets there, so they will already be on their way to a successful start with their new friend.

Here are a few to get you started.

- When you come home from school, remember to put your bags away and change your clothes before you talk to the dog.

- Treat the dog as you would like to be treated. Don't pull their ears or tails. Never shout at them.

- Always call the dog to you to pet it and don't go to the dog.

- It is not nice to look the dog in the eyes; he may take it as an invitation to fight.

- Don't go near his tail, don't pull it or step on it. He uses it to express feelings.

- Don't disturb a dog when he's eating, and never try to take his food away. He may defend it.

- When you play with him, don't pet him near his teeth. He may accidentally pinch your fingers.

- Never try to separate fighting dogs. Go and get help from an adult you know.

- Whether you are afraid or not, never run away from a dog – he'll take it as an invitation to chase you.

- You have two hands; he has only his teeth to hold on to you. Often you may think he wants to bite, but he may only want to hold on to you.

- Only play with a dog when you are with an adult.

- No two dogs are the same; you have to get to know them. Treat them kindly and gain their respect.

- If you see a dog outside, even if he looks kind, don't approach him.

- Never tease the dog with food or treats. Only give treats when an adult is present.

With the right personality, the relationship your kids can have with the dog can be something to cherish for the rest of their lives. However, it is not fair to a dog that has no interest in children to be subject to their behavior. As the pack leader, it is your responsibility to keep the pack happy and under control.

As a 12-year-old, Maggie can definitely give us some insight into growing up with her favorite dog.

DOODLE-ICIOUS: A HERMAN DOODLE DOG STORY

We welcomed the "bestest" ever Golden Doodle named Herman into our house in October 2004. He discovered the whole lower level of our house in a matter of minutes, due to the fact that he did not know how to move up and down the stairs. The next day, we decided to teach Herman about the wonders of the stairs. Though that was great at the time, it soon started not being the most wonderful thing. Herman learned to get into everything, and, like all puppies do, he learned to chew. He

chewed underwear, socks, bras, shoes, and pretty much anything he could get his paws on. He grew out of it eventually, though, and now he chews something only every now and then.

Our first Christmas with Herman was great. He received his very first present, a huge, gigantic bone that was lost in about the first 20 seconds after letting him outside with it. It is still buried to this day, or so we think, and nobody knows its whereabouts. Herman is now 3 years old, and is always making my family and me laugh. From playing "catch me", to being in the thick of all activities, to attending baseball and soccer games, to riding shotgun in our vehicles with his head and tongue hanging out the window, he is always doing something funny. Herman Doodle looks a lot like the shaggy dog except gold and a little bit of brown and white, and he has a more human personality rather than a dog personality. Herman is a truly wonderful, playful, and funny addition to our family. I love Herman and look forward to all our years growing up together.

Maggie Lyon
Lethbridge, Alberta

Not everyone adopts a puppy or an adult dog; some people do enjoy the company of a more mature dog. Here is a story from a gentleman about his experience with rescuing an older dog.

WHAT YOU CAN LEARN FROM TIME

I have always identified myself as an animal lover (a house is not a home without a little pet hair). Well, a few years ago, I decided to adopt a senior dog. I had done my share of time raising puppies, and now I was ready for a quieter beginning. While watching last year's "Super Bowl"

I had seen the Puppy Bowl, on Animal Planet, as well. They ran ads for Petfinder on the Internet as a great way to search for a new dog. So I went to www.petfinder.com and began my search. I spent hours roaming through the site and e-mailing rescue organizations about my selections before I found Sophie, a nine-year-old Border Collie. It was love at first sight. Sophie taught me many things.

Dignity – Sophie came from an abusive past. They found her with the wounds to make that assessment, as well as being flea-infested. She was wandering loose in Georgia. It took her almost a year to heal after I got her. She had only been at the rescue a few months before I found her. But she always held her head with a certain dignity, like a true Southern lady.

Kindness Still Exists – The man who found Sophie was kind enough to drive her two hours to a rescue center that would accept her. He also left them with a donation for her care. He is proof that kindness still exists in this world.

Joy – Anyone who has loved a pet knows joy. But Sophie came to me at a point in my life when having a four-legged to share TV time with was very special. We developed a kind of bond that not even a child, a parent, or a lover could fulfill.

Discipline – Sophie kept me in line like a classic drill sergeant. She seemed to love Frisbee, and everyday at five in the afternoon we would play. I learned to make sure I initiated the sessions. She might have been the drill sergeant, but I was the captain. Sophie spent four years trying to whip me into shape as a disc dog dad.

Persistence — *Somewhere in the midst of my relationship with Sophie I hit the big Five-O. Anytime that I wanted to despair about all that I hadn't done, I would look at Sophie. And realize that I still had a lot of quality time left in my life.*

Letting go is not giving up – *A year ago, I found a lump on Sophie's nose. I assumed she bumped it with the Frisbee. We had it checked out and spent five months of tests, surgery and drugs, but it was not going to get better. I decided to just keep her comfortable and happy. Sophie spent the next two months enjoying the warm days of spring with her face to the sun. Then, one night, she quietly died in her sleep. She and I had had each other for five years.*

Perspective – *She really affected my life, and I was able to reflect upon that during those last few months I had with her. I also started to let go of the worry and to focus on the good times we had.*

The value of taking risks – *I e-mailed the rescue when she died. About a month later I received another e-mail about a senior border Collie mix that had been left at rescue. Was I ready this soon? This dog was reported to be in her teens. I might not have long with her. Her name was Berta.*

Get a second opinion on items that are important – *Berta sits underneath my feet. I work out of my home. She is the best supervisor I have ever had. Anytime I ask her if it is time for a break, she agrees. We go outside for a toss of the Frisbee. Our vet says he can't see anything that would prove that she is in her teens. I don't really worry about her age, or mine. Instead, I just enjoy our time.*

Our friend in the previous story understands, as do I, that older dogs have as much to share with us as their younger counterparts. The reason the dog found itself in the shelter or rescue may not be behavior-related. There are many other reasons older dogs become homeless: death of a guardian, not enough time for the dog, change in work schedule, new baby, need to move to a place where dogs are not allowed, kids going off to college, allergies, change in lifestyle, prospective spouse doesn't like dogs. The list can go on.

If you choose to adopt an older dog, then there are advantages to consider, too. Most have already been house-trained. They know how to leave the furniture, carpets, shoes, and other "chewables" alone. They get along with humans and, in most cases, other dogs – and even cats in some cases. Older dogs, especially those that have known it before, appreciate love and attention. Finally, older dogs are easy to assess for personality. You will know how strong of a personality they have, and you also do not have to guess how big they'll grow.

By adopting an older dog, we can share in the compassion and the value of all life at all ages. We will also not be adding to the indiscriminate and inhumane breeding of dogs, whether it is for profit or to "teach the children about birth". And, of course, just as a puppy has his whole life ahead of him, so does an older dog have the rest of his life in front of him. You can give that older dog the best years of his life while, at the same time, bringing a wonderful addition into your family. Another consideration is the larger goal of helping end needless euthanasia. Adopting a dog who would be otherwise euthanized just because of his age, you can help prevent that from happening.

The older rescue is ideal for a household with very young children: the dog's personality is known and house-training does not have to be undertaken at the same time diapers need to be changed. Some convalescent and nursing homes make arrangements for pets to come and live with their owners, knowing the therapeutic value and the sense of loss to both patient and pet when they are separated.

So whether you choose a puppy or a rescue or an older dog, do your research into what you really want for your lifestyle. Make sure you understand the breed, but do not get fooled into the stereotypes. Remember that with the right signals all dogs can be happy, relaxed, and stress-free. Getting any dog is not something that should be taken lightly, because they will become members of your pack for the next 5, 10, 15 years of your life. It is also very important to remember when you get a new pet to update your Last Will and Testament to include provisions in case something happened to you. Many people think that a family member will simply take the animal. Rescue organizations are filled with dogs that families did not want. This is most certainly not what anyone of us would want to happen to our beloved canine companion.

Let's continue on our quest to improve our lives and the lives of the dogs among us.

"To get up each morning with the resolve to be happy...is to set our own conditions to the events of each day. To do this is to condition circumstances instead of being conditioned by them."
– Ralph Waldo Emerson

Condition circumstances. What does that mean? For one thing, it means you have the power to create your life. You are bringing the situations or circumstances into your life with your feelings. You can choose to move in a negative direction or in a positive one. The key is *you choose.* Our friend from the last story chose to enjoy each day and to make the days special with the dogs he rescued. We can all learn from that.

"Don't worry. Be happy."

– Meher Baba, Indian spiritual leader (1894-1969),
quote popularized in a song by Bobby McFerrin, 20th-
century American songwriter and performer

To have anything you want in your life, you must *be* and *feel* happy now! Expectations are powerful. If you expected it, it will happen. So, expect the things you want. If your dogs have issues and are fighting, and you expect that, then that is what you will get. If you expect peace, your vibrations along with your actions will bring you peace. If you expect to come home to a grumpy spouse, then that is the vibration you are putting out. Likewise, if you expect a bad day at work, that is what the universe will give you, exactly what you expect. I always expect success. Any failure I have is simply another step toward my success. I can always stay in control of situations when that is what I expect.

As the leader, it is important to keep that happy and in-control feeling. Remember to reward behavior you want, and smile when you see someone you love. This will go for miles in your relationships, especially with your children. Project the thought that "things always work out for you" because they always do, one way or another. Security is really just a myth, anyway. Realize today, this very moment, is the most important time. Dogs know that danger may lurk around every corner, and it does for us, too. That never stops their tails from wagging, though. Enjoy your time with the dog or the person you are with, before you move on to the next task.

Look at your relationships. Are you happy and in control? Or are things moving in the wrong direction? We often get caught up in ourselves and forget about other parties involved. We forget to look at things from their point of view. Sometimes we take the wrong attitude. Forward progress requires, you to see other perspectives. Walk a mile in their shoes before you judge.

As we have progressed through this book, I have presented you with many stories of how dogs can teach us the things we need in life. Of course, you can learn these things in other arenas as well. All animals have something to teach us, as do those great people who have come before us. Some of them I have quoted in this book to add emphasis to the lesson. As we move into the last chapter and our time together is coming to an end, I hope your awareness has begun to expand. We can all grow, and I have grown in the writing of this book. Life is full of kindred spirits to help guide us, and I am happy to call the dogs my teachers and guides.

CHAPTER
– *Ten* –

Lessons Learned
– *Living in Harmony with a*
Fulfilled Dog

CHAPTER
– *Ten* –

Success is a direction you choose. When you have issues with your dog, you have two ways to proceed, positive or negative. The same is true in our professional and personal relationships. You can choose to move in a negative direction or you can choose a positive direction. You will be amazed as you begin to watch people and they get a positive direction from you. They are often taken aback and not sure how to proceed.

As we move to successfully living in harmony with our dogs, we will have to take a look at our relationship with them.

Earlier in the book, we spoke about your paradigms being your beliefs, your conditioning. Old conditioning needs to change if you want to succeed. If you have always done something the same way but are not getting the results you want, you must look inside yourself for change. Maybe your perspective is not allowing you to see the whole picture. Therefore, look at things from a different view. Again, if you are having trouble with your dog, stop thinking, "Why doesn't he listen to me?". Instead, realize you may not be listening to him. Are you giving him the right signals? You may be giving off negative feelings, or you might be very concerned about a work project. It does not matter what you are feeling, if it is a negative emotion, then your dog does not care why and neither does the universe. You will simply get more negative results. It could also simply be that it is just not the right time yet. You may need to keep working on things until you see a difference. Think about the Law of Gender when you feel the time should have brought you your results already.

"Learn to become still, and take your attention away from what you don't want and all the emotional charge around it and place the attention on what you wish to experience.... Energy flows where the attention goes."
– Michael Bernard Beckwith

BE AWARE

Ask yourself: what you are thinking and what you are feeling? This will focus you on the moment and increase your awareness. Remember to be grateful and express gratitude. It is much nicer to meet people who act this way, and you will be surprised just how much you get back when you have an attitude of gratitude.

VISUALIZATION

This is a powerful tool. By working with the Law of Attraction you can generate your thoughts into things. It goes back to expectations. If you think it, you will achieve it.

After a day is over, review it in your head. Did it go the way you would have liked? Replay it the right way. We are all going to stumble and we can all improve. The universe is going to give us more opportunities for practice. Use this nightly routine and you will be ready for the next lesson.

When you have a dog with certain issues, you have to learn to work toward the end result of changing that issue. Taking the proper action is as important as having the proper thinking.

"Focus on the solution, not the problem."
– Walter Anderson

When you encounter a problem in life, or with your dog, focus on what you want – the solution. If your current results are not where you want to be and you are doing the right action, then look at where you want to go for improvement. Anyone that drives a car or rides a motorcycle knows that if you want to get safely to your destination, you need to look ahead. If you are looking down at where you currently are, your eyes are off the goal. You also should remember that it will take time to progress toward your goal. When you have a difficult project at work, do not get caught up in the results of the moment. You often cannot see the progress. This reminds me of the great story about water hyacinths in Jeff Olson's book, *The Slight Edge*. He describes the beauty of a delicate plant, that floats on pond surfaces in warm climates across the globe. They bloom over the course of 30 days. On the first day, no blooms are noticeable, and still not many on the 15th day. Two thirds into the month, you may notice only a small dense patch, and on the 29th day only half of the pond's surface is covered. But on the 30th day, the pond is blanketed by the water hyacinths. No water is visible at all.

If you constantly get caught up in saying, "My dog is so bad", "My dog has separation anxiety", "My dog barks at everything", my dog, my dog, my dog – you have not made room for your goal. You are also focusing on the things you do not want. You will achieve your goal by focusing on what you do want. When you look back on past problems, you just bring more problems to you now. Do not hold a grudge. It only holds you back. You want to create positive feelings.

Act As If

If we feel and act as if we are successful, that is the vibration we put out. This is going to help your dog if you give him the feelings he needs to improve. You are not pretending you don't have a problem. You know you do, but the focus is on the way you want things to be. This is the same principal when you want more money, or a better job or a better life. Recognize that there may be a problem, but look ahead to the end result.

Look for the positives in your dogs, your spouse, your friends, etc. Think about all the good things. When you keep this focus and are also taking the right action, then you get the result you want. I have repeated the same thing quite a lot in this past section, focus on what you want. The reason is because it is a very important step.

"Many people in Western culture are striving for success. They want the great home, they want their business to work, and they want all these outer things. But having these things does not necessarily guarantee what we really want, which is happiness. So we go for these outer things thinking they're going to bring us happiness, but it's backward. You need to go for the inner joy, the inner peace, and the inner vision first, and then all of the outer things appear."
– Marci Shimoff

Changes

In the process of living in harmony with our dogs, realize that if certain things change, then the pack may change, or even break up, as well. In the wild, that could mean the alphas were killed or injured. Change is what life is all about whether we like it or not. Whether it is our children growing up, our parents growing old, our health, or our career, things change. Sometimes the family breaks up, sometimes the job breaks up, and sometimes friends break up. If we do not roll with it and keep the right feelings and vibrations, our outcomes will be less successful. We will not live to the fullest.

When I was going through my rough times, I realized I could not give anything to anyone else. I really had nothing to give. Personal and family relationships suffered. All I could do was to take care of the animals in my sanctuary. If I had stayed focused on those depressed feelings, I would have gotten more of them.

First, it is important to feel good before you give anything out. Allow yourself to feel good. It is the only way to stay balanced. Then you can give out good because you will have it in stock. It really all started with a simple decision.

Once you allow yourself to feel good, you may be amazed at how quickly you do feel good. Start by saying things like, "Ah, what a relief", or "You know, maybe I can have this or do that." How about, "Now that's possible". These sentences help to remove negativity.

In other areas of your life, learn to allow and accept. When someone offers to buy you lunch, do not feel offended or challenged. Those are negative vibrations creeping in. This causes resistance to receiving money in other ways, since you are putting out a hesitation to receiving money. So, next time someone offers to buy lunch, be grateful and accept and say, "Thank you".

You can apply the same lesson to your love relationships, as well as to your dog or your work. If you had a bad day or a bad date, or a bad experience, don't continually talk about it. You will be causing your subconscious mind to focus on that and bring you more of it. Release the day, date, or episode, and look forward to the next positive, successful one you will have.

BE THE LEADER

Remember that leaders don't get miffed, they remain calm. Be calm. It is that simple. I know I have repeated this numerous times, but the first "C" in leadership is a real important one. It helps with canine confrontations, people confrontations, and job confrontations. When we make the right decision during an interaction with people or dogs, we gain trust. Not only will our dogs trust us, but we also trust ourselves. It goes back to the confidence we spoke about earlier. This keeps you feeling happy, and the confidence keeps you in control. It is easy to see how it will help your spouse or your boss as well.

Keep attitudes in check. Our thoughts, beliefs, and actions are all factors of success with ourselves, our dogs, and our lives. If things are not going the way you want, stop and look inside yourself at what you are really thinking. What do you believe is really going to happen? Look back at the actions you have been taking and adjust them if you need to.

In life, risk and resistance will never end. We must always keep pursuing and growing to stay on top. These are just some of the speed bumps in life asking if we really want something. We must learn to move from a reactionary mindset to a responsive one. Then you can successfully handle these bumps. Do the best job you can at anything you do. We become great by doing little things every day in a great way. This is our path to becoming the chosen leaders of our pack. You will also find that it is the path feeling fulfilled and thus, your accomplishments will have a special value.

"What is important is not what happens to us, but how we respond to what happens to us."
– Jean-Paul Sartre

We definitely learn as we go, and learning to respond to situations takes time. We need an increased awareness to realize the immediate reactions that may be starting. If we develop patience to wait until it is time to respond, our results will be far greater. Think back again to the Law of Rhythm. Claire Bennee's story shares her experience with the difficulty of reacting to a situation and some pretty harsh results.

IF ONLY I KNEW THEN WHAT I KNOW NOW

I love to travel; I had been working summer and winter seasons for a number of years. Therefore, I could not have any responsibilities such as pets. I dearly missed having pets because I love animals more than anything else. Then I settled in the United Kingdom and started studying veterinary nursing and working in a clinic. I made friends with a vet of the same age, Charlie. We rented a place together and thought it would be great to get a dog from one of the shelters…I mean, what better owners could he or she wish for, I thought?

Then Jakey came into our lives…a stunning young Dalmatian, which we loved to bits. We took him for runs in the fields, and he was full of life. One day, he ran off and refused to return; he was chasing sheep and was out of control. After about five hours and I don't know how many dead sheep, we got him back and gave him a good telling off. We didn't want it to happen again or for him to get shot by the farmers. So we decided it was best he be put to sleep, the hardest and most regretted decision of my life. It's incredibly hard for me to write about this now, because he was perfect and healthy.

Of course, life went on, and I needed a change. I found it hard to live with myself. I continued my studies on farms in New Zealand, and couldn't bear the thought of having more animals to call my own. There was just no way I was a worthy owner. As things turned out, I had a car accident and had to cut my trip short and come home. My parents were living in Spain at the time, so I went there and started to recuperate. The village where they live is gorgeous; if you're a nature lover like I am, then you would be in your element. Yet, there was something missing.

One day, on a walk in the countryside, I saw some horses grazing and stopped to admire them. I continued on my way and bumped into a man walking his dogs. He was also the owner of the horses. His name was Juan, and we became friends. I was new in the village and didn't know anybody; also, my Spanish wasn't brilliant at that time. Despite how hard I tried to not become attached, I kept being drawn back to him and his animals, even though I wasn't the settling down type and was already planning my next adventures.…

The time approached for me to move on, but I couldn't do it. I knew if I left it would be another very bad decision and I couldn't handle that a second time. So I stayed here with Juan and I started to learn about natural horsemanship, which then helped me discover dog listening. In the beginning, it hurt to be around Juan's animals. I felt I had no right; I was a fake who knew nothing. But, five years later, we now have three horses and five dogs that I adore. I know they've changed my life for the better. It has changed my life because I now feel at peace with myself, and whenever I need cheering up or have doubts, I know being with the animals will make everything better in life. I can look at the situation from a different, better perspective and respond accordingly.

Every dog I encounter teaches me something new, be it good or bad. I learn something from my own dogs everyday; with animals you never stop gaining knowledge. I endeavor to create an environment where an animal learns from me and teaches me as well.

My career is now as an alternative animal behaviorist. I studied vet nursing, animal communication with Amelia Kinkade from the United States, natural horsemanship, animal behavior, dog listening, and I am also studying to become an animal Bach Flower remedy practitioner and homeopath. But it's mainly the dog listening that brings me the greatest rewards, because now I help save "last chance" dogs and hope Jakey is looking down from heaven and smiling.

I will continue my animal-related studies because I feel this is what I am on earth for. I've found my path. If it hadn't been for Jakey, none of this would have happened, and because of Amichien Bonding, I have been able to regain confidence in myself and my capabilities with dogs. Like they say, everything happens for a reason.

Claire Amanda Bennee, Southern Spain
Dog Listener

"We must not, in trying to think about how we can make a big difference, ignore the small daily differences we can make which, over time, add up to big differences that we often cannot foresee."
– Marian Wright Edelman

Again, doing little things leads to greatness, and learning to respond rather than react will get you much further in life.

PERSISTENCE

Understand that persistence is the most important mental muscle we can develop. This next quote is a lesson to take with you in every area of your life. It is something to remember when you deal with those persistent dogs we have talked about.

"Fall seven times. Stand up eight."
– Japanese proverb

A Dog Listener commented that she looks upon her persistent dog as a challenge! "He's taught me so much, and the biggest lesson is it can't be rushed and will take as long as it takes!" When you are with your dog every day, it is hard to realize the progress that you both make. On the other hand, it is a process that happens quickly at times. It will depend on your dog's personality, as well as your abilities and willingness to grow. A lesson to remember…

"Nothing in this world can take the place of persistence. Talent will not; nothing is more common than unsuccessful people with talent. Genius will not; unrewarded genius is almost a proverb. Education will not; the world is full of educated derelicts. Persistence and determination alone are omnipotent. The slogan 'press on' has solved and always will solve the problems of the human race."
– Calvin Coolidge

FULFILLED LIFE

After recapping much of what I have learned from dogs, I will share a list of ways to look at life with your dogs. These are the attributes I see in a great owner who has a deep connection with their dog.

- Have empathy. Give your dogs what *they* need and not what you feel, as human instinct dictates, *you* need.

- Have that special relationship with your dog without being domineering or harsh.

- Work with your dog and not against him. Drop the prong, shock, choke collars, and head devices.

- Respect your dog for the species that it is, rather than using the term "stupid dog" or "just a dog".

- Understand your limits, and if you cannot give the dog 100%, then look for their best interest.

- Lead by example and not by intimidation. Remember dogs have more friends because they wag their tails, not their tongues.

- Put your dog first, not the TV program or the newspaper.

- Have an open mind to learning and don't be stuck in antiquated, abusive ways of the past.

- Have courage under fire. Remember to keep your head when all others are losing theirs.

- Have patience and let go of the quick temper, short fuses and frustrated reactions.

- Shoulder the blame instead of blaming it on the "bad" dog.

- Be aware; think ahead instead of getting caught off guard.

- Have fun instead of living life in a box, whether it is a mental one or a physical one.

- Rise to the occasion instead of stagnating with the masses.

- Have gratitude that this dog has chosen you, don't take the dog for granted.

- Learn how to use the will. Gain their respect willingly instead of taking it by force.

- Respond to the situation rather than react to it. There is a huge difference.

- Take action. Make decisions instead of sitting back idle.

- Share life with your dogs instead of owning them for your life.

- See the value that dogs have for us instead of only seeing us as a value for dogs.

- Be positive and feel good about your dog instead of complaining that your dog is not this or not that.

- *Never* underestimate your dog's instincts by thinking you always know best.

- Realize the dog is a different species instead of giving it what the human species needs.

- Know when to say goodbye and let your special friend rest... Don't be selfish and hold on while they are in pain.

- Let your dog be a dog instead of making it into a little human.

- Give the dog the best of yourself instead of what's left at the end of the day.

You can take almost every one of these statements and substitute the word spouse, parent, child, employee, etc. In doing these things in all areas of our life, we will receive better results.

I want to quote again from Marc Bekoff because his sentiments mirror the exact way I feel: "Animals are subjective beings who have feelings and thoughts, and they deserve respect and consideration. We don't have the right to subdue or dominate them for our selfish gain to make our lives better by making animals' lives worse." Marc goes on to express that as humans we know what suffering is and we must reduce it whenever we can: "By making decisions that help animals, we add compassion, not cruelty to our world."

Fulfillment in life requires awareness. I hope I have now made you aware! I would like to share two very inspirational quotes from the highly respected leader Mohandas K. Gandhi:

"First they ignore you, then they ridicule you, then they fight you, and then you win."

People have accepted many harsh ways of living with the animals as the norm. Be strong in your endeavor to help change the ways we look at and treat our dogs. Realize you may face the ridicule, but for your dog's sake, it is worth it.

And the second:

"The morality of a nation can be judged by the way a society treats their animals."

They all have something to share with us, teach us. Should we be so ignorant as to turn a deaf ear because we think we have all the answers?

MY JOURNEY OF DISCOVERY HAS BECOME A JOURNEY OF UNDERSTANDING

When striving for success in our lives, we must begin by understanding ourselves. When striving for success with dogs in our lives, we must begin with them. When we bring the two together, we can benefit by understanding our dogs. We give them respect by conveying to them that we understand their language. In doing this, we are allowing the dogs of our lives to reach back out to us and bring us closer to nature. They give us the gifts to grow in our own personal development to achieve a higher level of self. They show us how to be the best mothers, fathers, siblings, bosses, employees, and friends. They show you how to be the best you that you can be.

This journey is different for each individual owner and dog, and no two courses will be the same. Many will cross paths or ride alongside of one another, others will be oceans apart. A journey with one of your dogs may be very different from the journey with the other one. In the end, the result you are always looking for is the same – a content and happy soul walking with you on the journey of life.

I hope you have enjoyed our travel together and would welcome the opportunity to hear your personal stories of life lessons learned from your dogs, as well as from your other animal friends. I look forward to traveling with you all again very soon in the next book, *Tails of Change*. If you would like to join us in the wonderful ranks of Dog Listeners, please feel free to e-mail, write, or call. I would be more than happy to guide you to a better direction for your dog. I welcome the opportunity to speak to groups, to continue to reach more people and their canine companions. I will leave you with a passage from Buddha to ponder.

"Do not believe in anything simply because you have heard it. Do not believe in anything simply because it is spoken and rumored by many. Do not believe in anything simply because it is found written in your religious books. Do not believe in anything merely on the authority of your teachers and elders. Do not believe in traditions because they have been handed down for many generations. But after observation and analysis, when you find that anything agrees with reason and is conducive to the good and benefit of one and all, then accept it and live up to it."
– Buddha

THE AUTHOR

KIM KAPES

Born in the Pocono Mountains of Pennsylvania, Kim received her Bachelor's degree from Susquehanna University in 1990. She studied Psychology, with an emphasis on learning and behavior. Kim moved to Virginia where a career as a firefighter gave her the opportunity to train in emergency animal rescue. She became certified in that field and eventually relocated to Florida.

Kim is a recommended "Dog Listener", having traveled to England to certify with the renowned "Dog Listener" and author Jan Fennell. The owner of Wolf Song K9 Relations, she has helped companion dogs and their owners as well as rescue dogs from across the country. She is currently helping owners and their dogs in Orlando, Florida.

Kim spent time working with zoo animals to gain further experience. In addition to her canine relations work, she is the director of In Harmony with Nature animal haven. Her nonprofit organization is dedicated to helping animals in need. Plans are in the works for future expansion of the rescue to facilitate greater education, conservation, awareness, rehabilitation, and to be able to place more animals in loving homes.

PLEASE VISIT...
WWW.FROMWAGSTORICHESBOOK.COM

AS WELL AS...
WWW.INHARMONYWITHNATURE.ORG

**All the author's proceeds from the sales of this book benefit the animals of the sanctuary.

INDEX

A

B

C

E

F

G

H

P

Q

R

S

T

U

V

W

Y

Z

OTHER BOOKS FROM LifeSuccess Publishing

You Were Born Rich

Bob Proctor
ISBN # 978-0-9656264-1-5

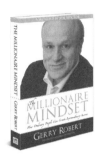

The Millionaire Mindset
*How Ordinary People Can
Create Extraordinary Income*

Gerry Robert
ISBN # 978-1-59930-030-6

Rekindle The Magic In
Your Relationship
Making Love Work

Anita Jackson
ISBN # 978-1-59930-041-2

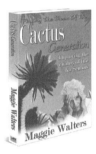

Finding The Bloom of
The Cactus Generation
*Improving the quality of
life for Seniors*

Maggie Walters
ISBN # 978-1-59930-011-5

The Beverly Hills Shape
The Truth About Plastic Surgery

Dr. Stuart Linder
ISBN # 978-1-59930-049-8

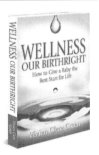

Wellness Our Birthright
*How to give a baby the best
start in life.*

Vivien Clere Green
ISBN # 978-1-59930-020-7

Lighten Your Load

Peter Field
ISBN # 978-1-59930-000-9

Change & How To
Survive In The New
Economy
*7 steps to finding freedom
& escaping the rat race*

Barrie Day
ISBN # 978-1-59930-015-3

Stop Singing The Blues
10 Powerful Strategies For Hitting The High Notes In Your Life

Dr. Cynthia Barnett
ISBN # 978-1-59930-022-1

Don't Be A Victim
Protect Yourself
Everything Seniors Need To Know To Avoid Being Taken Financially

Jean Ann Dorrell
ISBN # 978-1-59930-024-5

A "Hand Up", not a "Hand Out"
The best ways to help others help themselves

David Butler
ISBN # 978-1-59930-071-9

Doctor Your Medicine Is Killing Me!
One Mans Journey From Near Death to Health and Wellness

Pete Coussa
ISBN # 978-1-59930-047-4

I Believe in Me
7 Ways for Woman to Step Ahead in Confidence

Lisa Gorman
ISBN # 978-1-59930-069-6

The Color of Success
Why Color Matters in your Life, your Love, your Lexus

Mary Ellen Lapp
ISBN # 978-1-59930-078-8

If Not Now, When?
What's Your Dream?

Cindy Nielsen
ISBN # 978-1-59930-073-3

The Skills to Pay the Bills... and then some!
How to inspire everyone in your organisation into high performance!

Buki Mosaku
ISBN # 978-1-59930-058-0